From Special to Ordinary Schools

Case Studies in Integration

Neville Bennett and Allyson Cass

CASSELL

Cassell Educational Limited
Artillery House
Artillery Row
London SW1P 1RT

First published 1989

British Library Cataloguing in Publication Data
Bennett, Neville, *1937–*
   From special to ordinary schools: case studies in
   integration.
   1. England. Schools. Students with special needs.
   Integration.
   I. Title   II. Cass, Allyson
   371.9′046′0942

ISBN 0–304–31800–0 (hardback)
      0–304–31557–5 (paperback)

Phototypesetting by Activity Ltd. Salisbury, Wilts.
Printed and bound in Great Britain by
The Camelot Press, Southampton.

Contents

Introduction

The Warnock Report (1978) described integration as the central contemporary issue in special education, and this theme was strongly represented in the 1981 Education Act. It replaced the old categories of handicap, defining special educational needs as individual learning difficulties to be assessed by a multi-professional team. LEAs had to ensure special educational provision where it was needed, and to arrange such provision for those children for whom a statement was prepared and maintained. This provision was to be made in ordinary schools provided that this was compatible with the child's educational needs, the efficient education of other children and efficient use of resources. The rights of parents to have their views taken into account in the assessment process were substantially increased. However, the Act was brought into operation with no specific allocation of additional government funds.

Since that time the implications of the Act, and its implementation, have been analysed (see Welton *et al.*, 1982; Education, Science and Arts Committee, 1987), and a commitment to an integration principle has underpinned most significant texts on special educational needs. Much less analysed have been the act of integration itself, and its effects on those principally involved, the children and their parents; or the perceptions of those professionals who instigate, support and sustain the act—teachers, educational psychologists and advisers. There is a dearth of information on the curriculum and teaching approaches that newly integrated children experience, and on their experiences of their socialization into the new school setting. As McCall (1983) argued in relation to the lack of knowledge of appropriate learning environments, their specification must be based on speculation. McCall concluded, 'it is hoped that resources will be made more readily available … for experimental endeavours in this vital area'.

The main purpose of the study reported here was to provide knowledge of the process and outcome of integration, not for the purpose of generalization, but in an attempt to delineate the major issues involved, so that those participating in future acts of integration may be forewarned or better informed and thereby may be forearmed. An attempt has been made to provide a holistic picture by showing the actual experiences, social, emotional and intellectual, of five children who were previously categorized as

ESN-M, as they transferred from special into ordinary schools, together with a record of the attitudes and perceptions of the professionals involved, the children and their parents, to present the necessary multiple perspectives.

A second purpose was, following the implementation of the Education Act in 1983, to ascertain the administrative, procedural and policy decisions made in LEAs that could impact on acts of integration. This information was deemed critical to a fuller understanding of the wider issues since it is in these varying policy contexts that such professionals as educational psychologists and advisers strive to implement the Act. The focus here was on the attitudes, perceptions and experiences of such groups, the constraints within which they worked, and the impact of those constraints on the enactment of the legislation.

Accordingly the study was carried out in two phases. In phase 1 the principal educational psychologists and the advisers with responsibility for special education were interviewed in seventeen local education authorities. These LEAs were contained within a geographical area bounded by the Scottish border to the north, the Pennines to the east and the River Mersey to the south. This area was deliberately chosen for its diversity. LEAs varied from county to metropolitan borough, from large to small, and served populations ranging from predominantly rural to urban.

The interviews were normally carried out in the interviewees' offices, and were tape recorded for later transcription and analysis. Each interview covered the same six basic issues and utilized the same set of open-ended questions developed on the basis of pilot work carried out elsewhere. Each question was followed up by a probe where necessary, and once the basic issues had been covered the agenda was opened up and led by the interviewee.

The questions put to the educational psychologists covered the following areas:

1. Identification of children with special educational needs.
2. The referral system.
3. Statements—advantages and disadvantages.
4. Future policy.
5. Developments in primary and secondary schools.
6. Advice and support services.

Questions for the advisers related to the following six issues:

1. Integration—the authority's policy and the influences and constraining factors that affect it.
2. Statements—the adviser's views and the authority's priorities in preparing these.
3. Future policies in relation to statements and integration.
4. Developments in primary and secondary schools.
5. Attitudes of primary, secondary and special school teachers.
6. Transfer from special to ordinary school—monitoring of performance.

The opportunity also arose to discuss some of these issues with those administrators responsible for taking the final decisions on children's placements. These opportunities were always taken since, although they were outside the original research brief, they added another pertinent perspective.

The six issues served as the basic analytic framework for the interviews, the results of which are portrayed in Chapters 1 and 2. These chapters provide the necessary administrative and policy backdrop to the acts of integration considered in later chapters.

In phase 2 five children were followed through the process of transferring from special (ESN-M) to ordinary schools. They were chosen opportunistically, i.e. they happened to be the children transferring at that particular time. There were three boys and two girls. Three transferred at the age of 11 and two at 14, all to comprehensive schools. The aim of following these children through the final term of their special school and the first year of their ordinary school was to acquire a better understanding of the salient issues in that process from the perspectives of the different actors—children, teachers and parents—as well as to make some assessment of the quality of their academic and social experiences.

We have been studying the quality of children's learning experiences at different ages and in different settings over the past seven years (Bennett *et al.*, 1984, 1987; Bennett and Kell, 1989). Our approach to learning is constructivist in origin, derived from insights provided by cognitive psychology. In this conception learners are active and interpretive, and learning is a covert, intellectual process providing the development and restructuring of existing conceptual schemes. Teaching affects learning through the pupil's thought process, i.e. teaching influences pupil thinking, pupil thinking mediates learning.

Intended classroom learning is embedded in the curriculum tasks or activities that teachers present to children (or allow them to choose), and the activities of the learner on these tasks are crucial to their development. Thus, in order to understand classroom learning, it is necessary to observe children's performances on their tasks, and to ascertain the extent to which the demand in their assigned or chosen work is appropriate or matched to their capabilities. Since learning takes place in complex social settings, it is also necessary to assess the impact of social processes, such as grouping arrangements, peer exchanges and adult–child interactions, on children's classroom experiences.

The findings from the studies undertaken from this perspective are clear-cut and uniform—a high proportion of tasks provided for high attainers underestimate them, and an equally high proportion of tasks for low attainers overestimate them. Identical findings to these were also reported in various HMI surveys (1978, 1983, 1985). In the 9–13 middle school survey HMI argued that 'both the more able and less able were not given enough suitable activities in a majority of schools', and in the 8–12 middle school survey they similarly argued that 'overall, the content, level of demand and pace of work were most often directed towards the children of average ability in the class'.

The implications of these patterns seem clear: providing work that is too easy for high attainers will not stretch them academically, and providing work that is too hard for low attainers is likely to block academic progress. Although both are unfortunate pedagogically, the latter appears to be the more serious in that progress is actually truncated, and is likely to be associated with a diminution in motivation.

The possible implications of these findings for children with special educational needs seem straightforward. Will children with learning difficulties who are integrated into ordinary schools suffer from being overestimated? What impact will that have on their progress and on their motivation? These were some of the questions that guided this multiple case study.

In each case the child was observed in the special school in the term before transfer. Observation focused on the children and their involvement in their tasks in mathematics and language lessons. Further observations and interviews with them were carried out to ascertain the extent to which these tasks were appropriate to their capabilities. In addition the children were interviewed about their work, their attitude to the special school and their views on their transfer. The teachers were interviewed about the children, their academic and social skills, the curriculum covered and their expectations of success in the ordinary school. The teachers also agreed to retain and provide samples of the children's work in order for us to gain an impression of curriculum covered and the quality of children's responses. Finally, in order to provide a historical context, each special school head-teacher allowed us access to all school records, including medical, psychological and teacher assessments, to enable the production of a school career profile. The same information was collected in the ordinary schools. Some of this was restricted to the first term although observations were also carried out throughout the third term, and in each case both the children and their teachers were interviewed at the end of the first and third terms. To complete the data collection both parents of each child were interviewed in their own homes in the third term after transfer in order to gain their perceptions of the academic and social integration of their offspring.

The findings of phase 2 are presented in Chapters 3 to 6. Chapter 3 introduces the children and their history of schooling; Chapter 4 records their curriculum experiences and the appropriateness of their work; Chapter 5 concerns the perspectives of the children and their teachers on their social and academic integration; and Chapter 6 presents the parents' perspectives. Finally, Chapter 7 summarizes the findings and relates them to contemporary thinking as expressed in, for example, the recent Select Committee report on the implementation of the 1981 Act (Education, Science and Arts Committee, 1987) and recent research evidence on the education of children with special educational needs.

Chapter 1

Integration: Policy and Constraints

INTRODUCTION

Few of the professionals we interviewed in the seventeen authorities saw the 1981 Education Act as having revolutionized ideas or practice concerning integration. This was because the ideological stance that all children should be educated in ordinary schools was embedded in conditions which served as either loopholes or safety valves, enabling authorities to make their own decisions concerning provision. Apart from the specification that account should be taken 'in accordance with Section 7, of the views of the child's parents', educating a child in an ordinary shool had to be compatible with

(a) his receiving the special educational provision that he requires;
(b) the provision of efficient education for children with whom he will be educated; and
(c) the efficient use of resources.

(Education Act, 1981, 2:3)

The following was thus a fairly typical comment: "I think the intention is there for integration, but nothing's made of it in the 1981 Act, it's not emphasized at all and I think it's a very poor vehicle of integration, very poor indeed.' Although in some authorities with low special school populations children with special educational needs were integrated, in those with extensive separate school provision the legislation imposed little real pressure on them to change. They had not been forced to retain children in primary or secondary schools and they were not forced to transfer those in special schools back into ordinary schools. No authority defined the prime objective of the review procedure as being to identify children ready to enter or re-enter ordinary school. Some expressed a hope that special schools would change as a result of the obligatory reviews and reassessments now demanded of them, but these had less to do with integration than with the establishment of clear aims and objectives in special schools. If children were re-integrated as a result of the review, then this was merely a side-effect of the process.

A view stressed was that if integration was to increase there was a need for primary and secondary schools to become more skilled and effective in educating children with special educational needs. Many with special educational needs already in those schools were seen as being inadequately catered for and advisers and educational psychologists were keen not to see an increase in integration without a comparable increase in the ability of ordinary schools to provide for them. If the cost of this was integration itself then it was clear that was the price many were happy to pay. These were professionals who were trying on very limited funding to improve the educational lot of children with special educational needs and what they did not want to see was separate special provision being run down and primary and secondary schools being left to cope as best they could. Their fear was that the schools would not cope and children with special educational needs would suffer as a result. Yet the one thing they saw as being a prerequisite to a successful integration in practice—the need for ordinary schools to change and develop—was not stressed in the Act, and on these grounds the Act was widely criticized. Nevertheless, this did not prevent some from using it to achieve this very purpose. One adviser stated: 'We are, I suppose, using the Act to a certain extent, to beat people over the head. I think the Act can be more or less what you want to make of it.' Another said succinctly: 'The Act will only be seen in retrospect to be successful in so far as the primary and secondary schools are able to respond to the needs of a wider number of pupils.'

INTEGRATION: LEA POLICIES

Attempts to make strict comparisons across authorities are very difficult because integration was differently defined in relation to populations of special needs and the extent of special provision in each LEA. Thus children with identical characteristics would be dealt with quite differently in different LEAs. In those LEAs where there was limited separate school provision, the child would remain in the ordinary sector, whereas in LEAs with better provision the same child would be in special school. As one psychologist noted, 'I look at youngsters who came from ESN-M schools in other authorities and we know we wouldn't have dreamt of putting them in an ESN-M school.' The situation was thus reminiscent of the days of secondary school selection where labelling, i.e. 11+ pass or fail, was determined as much by the extent of grammar school provision as by the child's test scores. In the area of special needs the labelling of children as being 'educationally subnormal' or as having 'moderate learning difficulties' has been and still is as dependent on provision as on the extent of the learning and/or social difficulties. Nevertheless, from the interviews it was possible to identify five groups of LEAs with regard to their policy stances.

Group 1: Policy of integration

The only LEA claiming to have a policy of integration did, nevertheless, take account of the possibility of a mismatch between policy and practice. 'The committee has taken on board the spirit of the Act, its policy is one of integration. Giving effect to it of course may be another matter.' Although at the time of interview it was clear that this policy would result in changes in provision, the exact nature of these was unclear. Provision for children with moderate learning difficulties was under review. However, this was not such a radical policy as might have been envisaged. The suggested change was from separate special schools to units within ordinary schools, i.e. locational, rather than functional, integration. The authority had recommended ordinary schools to review their policies 'to ensure that their remedial or special needs departments remain as open as possible', and an established unit at a comprehensive school was suggested as providing an appropriate model for future developments. It was not the authority's intention to close down all special schools. Their idea of integration involved pruning rather than the elimination of special schools. 'We are saying first and foremost that placement will be in a mainstream school. The question then is, "Is that an appropriate placement?" If the answer is "no", we seek an appropriate placement because the duty is to meet the child's needs.'

Group 2: Integration where possible

Three authorities claimed to have a policy of integration where possible. In one of these a number of changes had taken place before the 1981 Education Act. Separate special schools had been restructured into first and secondary schools, with transfer to the latter at the age of 13. Review procedures for children within special schools were established and part-time and short-term special school placements were introduced. The adviser stated: 'We see children being placed in special schools for one year, any special school for one year. At the end of that year, we review their progress and then either put them in a different school or return them to their ordinary school, or they have another year at the special school, but we encourage the notion that children are only placed for one year in the special school.' No further changes to the system were planned in this authority.

The second authority dated their policy of integration where possible back to 1971. The psychologist outlined their typical approach: 'As far as I'm concerned one starts off with the premise that all children should be educated within the ordinary system if possible and then you work through the "if possibles" and only when you find a "not possible" do you start talking about alternatives. That's a hierarchical view and it's a view we've always held and tried to put over.'

Although no single factor could be readily identified as affecting the decision to implement such a policy, the adviser thought that an important contributory factor might have been that too many children were being selected to go to ESN-M schools on the basis of poor reading quotients. Since then children have been selected on much wider criteria and tended to have a combination of difficulties. For those with less severe difficulties 'opportunity classes' had been established in ordinary primary schools, and teachers had been appointed over the staffing ratio. As a result of this, the authority had a particularly low special school population. Many children who in other authorities might have been receiving their education in special schools were being educated in ordinary schools. While some attention was to be devoted to the ordinary secondary school sector to encourage a whole-school approach in providing for children with special needs, no other changes were planned. The special school system was seen as providing for a 'population that would find it very difficult indeed to manage in an ordinary school'. In authorities such as this, children with moderate learning difficulties who were currently in the mainstream had never been extracted. The question of placing them in separate special school provision had therefore never arisen.

The policy adopted by the third authority in this group was that of Section 2 of the 1981 Education Act, and a policy document with a statement to that effect was sent out to ordinary schools. The adoption of an official policy had been accompanied by official changes in provision, the major one being the development of a special education advisory and support service at primary level. Others included in-school in-service training, the identification of teachers within the LEA as link teachers for special needs and improved links with support services. No specific plans had been developed regarding the authority's schools for children with moderate learning difficulties, but it was suggested that some changes would take place.

Group 3: Implicit policy of integration where possible

This is essentially a sub-group of group 2, the difference being that no policy decision had been taken, although these four LEAs 'fostered integration where possible'.

Neither policy adoption nor major changes in provision were planned in any of these authorities, although one had a working party looking at the whole question of integration and it was suggested that this might lead to a move from the use of special schools to special units within ordinary schools. In another the adviser argued that the adoption of a policy might not work in the interests of the child with special needs: 'I don't think I myself would be happy if [the authority] had a policy of integration. I think the temptation there is to say, "Well, okay, we do away with the ESN-M special schools totally and put all children into ordinary schools", which I think would present a big headache. I think the working arrangements we have at the moment work to the advantage of the child.'

In another authority within this group parents' wishes came first. Professionals advised parents, but ultimately the authority would go along 'in nearly every instance' with the parents' decision, whatever that decision might be. However, not all professionals within the authority were happy with this system. One psychologist argued, 'It could be construed as being positive, "oh, we're on the side of the parents" and "the children's welfare and the parents' welfare are primary considerations", but I don't think it's that at all. I think it's because the authority doesn't like to have policies.... If you've got an authoritarian system where the power is controlled by one or two people, then it's much easier if you can decide on an individual basis what should happen in a particular case.... If you've got a policy for it then the authority in a sense is dissipated because everyone says, "well, this is what we do in these circumstances" and if there's going to be an exception made it's got to be made on an exceptional basis.' He thus thought the absence of clear policy made for unfair practice. 'It leads to the parents who are, let's say, less educated, less articulate, less pushy, accepting what's given to them and the ones who, for one reason or another—not necessarily related to being articulate, but perhaps to the availability of a councillor or something like this—can put pressure on the people who make the decisions, who in our authority would be the administrators, then something will happen.'

As in a number of other authorities, a working party had been looking at special educational needs provision and, as seemed to be a common result of such parties, there were plans to move towards developing units in ordinary schools, with a concentration of resources for children with particular difficulties in particular schools—those schools that were 'able to cope better'.

In another authority within this group attempts to integrate children had been initiated by one or two of the special schools, as an adviser explained: 'Instances of children integrating into ordinary school really have been to do with the innovation of a particular school, a particular head and his relationships with the mainstream schools.' At authority level there was some interest in integration, but it had numerous special schools and any change was bound to be gradual if it occurred at all. Two working parties had looked at the possibilities for change in the education of children with moderate learning difficulties and of those with physical difficulties. It had been suggested that two areas within the authority might be selected as pilots for integration schemes.

Group 4: Policy not determined

None of the remaining authorities stated that they had a policy of integration. However, in giving accounts of practice it was difficult at times to see any real distinction between those who said they had policies and those who said they had not. The distinguishing feature often seemed to be that the former group were prepared to describe their practice as being official while the latter were not. The real distinction was not whether the authority said they had a policy, but whether, and to what degree, they had and used their special school provision.

One authority had a number of established integration schemes, but felt that policy was 'too big a word' to describe the steps they had taken towards this. Of the schemes established, that for the hearing-impaired was the most fully developed and was being used as a role model for an additional scheme to integrate children with moderate learning difficulties into the ordinary school. An extra teacher was to be appointed to each of the authority's schools for children with moderate learning difficulties to enable teachers to take on support duties in mainstream schools.

In another authority discussions were being held concerning the restructuring of the ESN-M and S schools and, to quote the adviser and principal educational psychologist for the authority, 'possibly closing them'. In her opinion there were too many places available in these two sectors of separate special provision.

Three authorities stated that they did not have a policy of integration but that their special school populations were, in any case, at a very low level. Working parties were looking at the whole area of special education in two of these. In one it was hoped that the group would establish 'what we see as being the developments we should be expected to make'. In the other it was expected that the group would suggest 'which direction the authority might take' and it was implied that the likely suggestion would be that the authority switch from separate special schools to units in ordinary schools. However, the principal psychologist in the authority was less than certain that this would ever become a reality, commenting that there was 'a lot of talk, but not much action. It's all empty words'.

In the third authority in this group children described as being marginally handicapped had been retained in the ordinary sector for the past seven years, causing a reduction in the authority's special school population. It was said that children currently in separate special school provision tended to be 'multiply handicapped in the sense that a very high proportion of them are very disturbed as well'. Thus the scope for integration into ordinary schools was thought to be very limited. This was a common comment made by advisers and psychologists in those authorities with low special school populations. Even so, although there were no plans within the authority to attempt to integrate this group, the authority was about to review its provision and changes of a minor nature were expected.

Group 5: Policy of no policy

In only one of the seventeen authorities was it stated categorically that the authority did not have a policy of integration and that no changes were planned or were likely 'in the near future'. The adviser explained: 'The authority has committed itself over the years to maintaining special schools. All authorities have.'

CONSTRAINTS ON INTEGRATION

When constraints were discussed the issue of resources emerged at the level of both the local authority and the school. But many other factors were felt to affect integration negatively. Prime among these were school organization, curriculum and the skills of teachers in primary, secondary and special schools.

Resources

Lack of finance was seen as a major constraint in most authorities. One adviser summed up the situation as follows: 'We just haven't got the money. We're talking about vast amounts of money. We're talking about advisers, peripatetic teachers, curriculum assistants for every kind of eventuality. In reality this authority, with 48 000 children, has got me. That's it!'

Those authorities that had invested heavily in separate special provision in the past faced a particularly difficult task if they wished to break out of this pattern. Having invested in separate provision they had little money to reallocate to, and thereby develop, a more integrated system. Ability or inability to draw in extra money to redistribute in other ways by withdrawing out of county placements was a subject raised in a number of authorities. One adviser commented: 'It is a constraint, because that is the whole question of the switch in resources, it would be very costly to change. Where we've had children who've been farmed out and we're bringing them back there is a saving and we can plough that back into an integration kind of policy.' In an authority where few children had been 'farmed out' the adviser commented: 'It was stated so categorically that it [integration] was to be done within existing financial resources. Our resources are desperately limited because we didn't have a lot of children outside the authority. We had a few at one school who perhaps could be brought back in and then we had children in schools for the maladjusted and the ESN in residential places, just one or two, and it's only in so far as one's able to reduce that kind of placement that a little bit of money comes back into the authority that can be reallocated.'

The difficulty in adopting a policy of integration was not only that no extra resources had been made available for children with special educational needs but also that those available to primary and secondary schools were under threat. As schools came under economic pressure, resources for special needs were seen to be one of the first areas to be squeezed. One psychologist described special educational needs departments as being 'Cinderellas of the school'. The adviser in this authority agreed that they were generally 'very vulnerable' but pointed out that whether or not they became the victims of cuts depended on two factors: the attitude of the head teacher and how persuasively the department could argue its case. The school's priorities in terms of funding were seen in most authorities as being the prime question. One principal educational psychologist commented: 'Sometimes as a consequence of falling rolls they're losing members of staff, protecting core departments if you like, and the remedial departments are under-funded and under-resourced. It's a question of priorities and if the priority is A-level they are not going to have much money left over for the remedial department.'

Nevertheless, not all professionals had sympathy with the view that the solution for schools was resources. One psychologist argued that the resources available to teachers were not fully exploited: 'I think the teaching profession have a lot to answer for when they say, "we can't" and "we haven't got the resources". I don't think they use their own intelligence enough to look at the needs of children right through their school and devise their own schemes. They expect authorities to make decisions for them. Very often the authorities expect head teachers to make professional judgements as to how they run their school, so you get a vacuum in the middle where nobody does anything.'

Some took a more balanced view, citing both lack of resources and poor organization of resources as major causes of educational failure. For example, one psychologist stated: 'We've got about the third worst primary pupil–teacher ratio in the country. And because of that we've got teaching heads.... Every one of our primary heads has a teaching timetable and I believe you've got to work on the primaries, you've got to get your primaries really keyed up and resourced up to meet special needs so that you're preventing educational failure. In this authority I'm afraid there is no hope of improving that. We've got very very few post-holders for special needs in primary schools, we've got very little expertise, there's tremendous ignorance about organizing resources, organizing the classroom, actually using post-holders in a professional way to lead their colleagues. You've got to get all that happening before you can start talking about a policy of integration because without that factor you're going to get kids failing, and teachers may have all the goodwill in the world, but actually won't know how to cope and there's nobody on the spot to help them.'

The view most frequently stressed was that primary and secondary schools needed to change and develop before integration could take place. Schools were often described as being unable or unwilling to adapt to children's needs, with secondary schools coming in for the greatest criticism. Primary schools, although not seen as entirely blameless, were generally viewed as being far more responsive to children's needs. One psychologist said: 'The large factory schools have become much more impersonal and management systems.... There's much more sympathy and support in the majority of primary schools. They will look after their weaker brethren. The secondary schools do not. You've got an organizational system which is based on specialist teaching. I get the kid who's not coping with English and reading and he's doing French. "Well," you say, "why can't you cut that out?" "Can't reorganize the timetable. Can't make exceptions for this kid." The teacher who would normally have taken them for withdrawal groups is committed to another group at that time, so the kid has got to go to French, come what may. And really head teachers and the whole hierarchy of management are very unsympathetic. They pay lip service. They retreat to the system and make their defences. We can't reorganize timetables, they're predetermined, we're short of staff, we haven't got good remedial departments. They're not really geared up to look after the remedial child.' Another principal educational psychologist commented: 'I mean there isn't any doubt that you can integrate at primary level. Even the lousiest school, the most formal school, you could integrate much more easily than you could in a secondary school.'

Curriculum

An exam-oriented curriculum, fed to those who would not be taking the exam as well as to those who would, was seen as being a major problem in secondary schools. Not surprisingly, secondary schools were accused of failing to follow a truly comprehensive philosophy. A psychologist argued: 'I suppose the concept of, or the idea of, comprehensivization in theory has meant that we now have schools which cater for children in a much wider range of abilities. That's the idea, but in practice you've still got schools flying their old flags, their old staff with the same philosophy, so the grammar schools are operating very much like grammar schools, secondary mods are behaving very much like secondary mods.' It was asserted that, rather than teachers devising suitable course material with children's needs in mind, they tended to use the same syllabus across the board, with less of it completed with lower attaining children, with less success. 'They've got to find ways of educating everybody' argued one adviser. A psychologist argued that improvements could be made if all teachers spent more time thinking about the curriculum: 'There's a lot of work been done on the curriculum over the last few years, a lot of reports have come out and my experience going round schools is that teachers have never heard of them, let alone looked at them, a lot of teachers. And if they would only start reading about the curriculum and thinking about the curriculum and discussing the curriculum they could improve the quality and standard of teaching in their schools'.

Not all agreed that the secondary school curriculum was inappropriate for children with special educational needs. One adviser argued that it was, but gave reasons why it did present a problem: 'I think this whole concern with curriculum is misplaced. If I could just ensure that the best teachers went to the children with learning difficulties, our problems would be over. I'm not saying that you always get the best teachers as heads of departments, but some of the best lessons I've seen for slow learners have been taken by heads of departments in subjects where you just wouldn't think it was possible. I am talking about very low attaining children doing cracking French and science lessons.... Your good teachers know their subjects, have good skills, manage very well. But you have to argue on the curriculum taken by the less able because it is a matter of fact that the less qualified, less able teachers end up taking the less able children.'

The inflexible structure within secondary schools and the inappropriacy of the curriculum for low attaining pupils was linked to the degree of skill and experience of teaching staff. Inappropriate teaching strategies and a general lack of skill and experience were seen as being major problems. One adviser described the situation in a mixed ability classroom: 'If you are going to teach geography and you're going to teach it to third-year children and you're going to teach the same thing to those 30 children, that's very simple and you've only got to keep one ball going up and down all the time, haven't you? You've got to keep 30 personalities occupied but you've only got to find work for one person. That's all the 30. That's simple. To get them to start throwing different balls and start juggling things and keeping things in their head, you're frightened to start.'

Another principal educational psychologist said: 'There's not enough skill. That's the biggest weakness in the system.... I think we're just about getting to a psychology of instruction, looking at what kids are up to, what the next step is and how you meet the next step, how you plan targets and how you introduce methods for teaching, what methods work, what methods don't. Really there's not an awful lot of skill. Teachers look at you wide-eyed when you start talking about the individual assessment, the child from the teacher's point of view, looking at a competent model of assessment. They say "oh yeah", and worry about getting to the butcher's before closing.'

As a result of concern over whether teachers could actually incorporate children with special needs into their classrooms and cater adequately for them, some voiced the fear that if integration did take place children with special educational needs would be ignored: 'In every class of 30 there's probably a couple of them can't read very well and the geography teacher gives them an essay to do at the end, tells them about the lesson and then says, "now write about it for me". And so those two can't write. Now they're your ESN-Ms, aren't they? So what do you do with them? Well, the teacher ignores them because they know if they ignore them for 35 minutes, which isn't a very long time, they go somewhere else, to another area, to another subject and the same thing probably happens to them there.... This is one of the things that really worries me. I think that so many of the ESN-M children really are remedial. I know in secondary schools in particular they're afraid that ESN children are going to be a problem, but most of them are very amenable and they will sit and accept being ignored. You'd feel a little bit more confident if you thought they were going to make demands on the teachers that *couldn't* be ignored and then they'd have to cater for them. There's a tremendous amount of, I was going to say in-service work [needed], but it's more radical than that.'

The need for more in-service training was stressed, while some pointed out the inadequacies of initial teacher training. One senior educational psychologist said of newly qualified teachers: 'Nobody in initial training is prepared for the range of difficulties that children have. It is just impossible for teacher training to do that. I think we have to acknowledge that people who come into teaching are barely prepared for the routine stuff with kids who cope.... I think if you wanted to incorporate a reasonable preparation for dealing with, say, the fact that 20 per cent of your population is going to have difficulties, you've virtually got to add another year on. If you ask people—primary trained teachers—how much time they spent on the teaching of reading, you would be lucky to find more than a week or two in three years. "How much time did you have on reading tests, spelling tests, that sort of thing?" "Hardly anything".'

Teachers' attitudes

Difficulties in resourcing ordinary schools in general and, in particular, in staffing them adequately were said to have a clear effect on teachers' attitudes towards integration. When teachers referred children to the psychological service, one psychologist argued: 'They're saying, "We're in a contractual situation, we're losing staff. We're finding it very hard to organize our remedial departments without having extra problems thrust on us. So, no, we can't manage them." The implications are there behind the statements that teachers make: "We can't cope with him and he can't cope with us. So you'd better do something about it." '

The following comment from one adviser was typical: 'I found that head teachers and their teachers are quite happy provided the resources are available and the teacher–pupil ratio is satisfactory. They say there's no way that they can take difficult children in any shape or form just as an addition to their present class numbers.'

The link between attitudes and resources was made by professionals in all authorities, including those in which children with moderate learning difficulties were already integrated and those which were planning integration. In an authority of the former type the adviser described teacher attitudes as being 'pretty good, considering the pressure'. In one of the latter type the adviser said that teachers had 'healthy anxieties about the authority's general intentions and their resource implications'. But ordinary school teachers' attitudes were said to be affected by other factors, such as their views on children's abilities, learning and what education was about. An adviser in an authority with a lot of special schools explained: 'Children are streamed in this authority, not now, but we had schools in this authority which streamed children by the way they looked. By the way they looked and by the clothes they wore they were put into As and Bs at the end of the week at school. So you can see it's going to be a change of attitude if the ESN-M world walks in. You know what streams they'd be in.'

Some of those interviewed held the view that teachers in primary and secondary schools laboured under gross misconceptions about children with special educational needs and the quality of separate provision. It was alleged that ordinary school teachers' perceptions of special children and special schools were hazy and frequently wrong. Children who attended special schools tended to be seen by ordinary school teachers as cases they would not be able to cope with: 'They have some sort of notion that there are terrible sorts of children out there that they won't be able to cope with and it's not like that at all.' Such lack of familiarity with children from special schools was said to be causing ordinary school teachers to be anxious and fearful of integration. One psychologist said simply: 'I think the attitude of teachers in the ordinary system is very much the attitude of anybody who is faced with a situation which he is not familiar with, and that's initial apprehension.' Similarly, an adviser who defined the fear of ordinary school teachers as being the biggest obstacle to integration said: 'Most of them have no knowledge of it, no experience of it, they've no training in it and therefore they have a certain fear of it.' One adviser described the attitude of ordinary school teachers as being one of 'let this cup pass from me'.

The nature and quality of separate special provision was another area open to misconception as the reality was that the disparity between the ordinary and the special schools' resources was not always as great as primary and secondary school teachers tended to assume. One psychologist argued: 'People say to us as psychologists, "this child needs the help of a special school", without having any idea of what help is available, and I know secondary heads don't like me saying this, but some of the secondary schools have geared up their resources in such a way that they are able to offer for maths and English work group sizes of eight—official time—and the kids would join in the other normal size classes. Now, you know, some of our special schools are offering class sizes of twelve, fifteen.'

In some authorities psychologists and advisers were trying to correct such mis-conceptions. For example, one, who was particularly critical of the separate authority special schools for children with moderate learning difficulties, encouraged the primary or secondary teacher of any child transferring to special school to go along with the child on his or her first day. The aim was for the ordinary school teacher 'to see what it's like'. It was a small scale bid to change teachers' opinions and attitudes. 'They have this idea that a special school is *really* special. It's not special at all. It's just a collection of pathetic kids being taught not very well by not very good teachers.... There's this very rigid way of working through whatever books they've got and not standing back and thinking about the skills of children, or how best to teach them, or the needs of those children. They just don't think in those terms.'

In no LEA were special school teachers said to be openly accepting integration. Their general response was said to be guarded and reluctant, arising partly from a concern over their own futures. They were aware that any changes in authority policy could mean redeployment for them. Moreover, they were aware that, if they were actually to support integration and make a concerted effort to reintegrate children already in their schools, they would be destroying their own roles in the system. Yet it was made clear that their attitudes were not entirely the product of self-interest. There was said to be a genuine concern among special school teachers that children who were integrated might not be adequately catered for in ordinary schools, and confidence in the ability of secondary schools in this respect was very low. As one adviser said, 'They are very very worried [that] the children who they perceive as having special educational needs are not going to have their needs met in the same way in the rough and tumble of the big comprehensive school as in their own small institutions.'

It was also noted that special school teachers were not oblivious of the disadvantages of segregating children. They were said to recognize the system they worked within as a socially divisive one, which isolated a minority and labelled them as being different from their peers. But they took the view that the problem would not be resolved simply by placing children with learning difficulties in ordinary schools. Although these children would be saved from carrying the special school label, they might still be the victims of teasing and bullying within the ordinary school. Awareness of the disadvantages of segregation was not something that automatically led special school teachers to assume a pro-integrationist line, because it was a perspective easily countered by other arguments.

The perception of reluctance and apprehension among special school teachers held true with the exception of those interviewed in two authorities, both of which had very small special school populations. The adviser for special education in one of these commented that: 'Because there's been about 40 school closures in [the authority], our separate system has been contracting and getting smaller and more beautiful and catering for a population that would find it very difficult indeed to manage in the ordinary school.' In the second authority the special school population had long been at a very low proportion: 'I would say that we have been implementing Warnock and the

1981 Act in this authority for years and years and years by comparison with any of the ones around us.... Our schools are handling youngsters who, had they been in [a neighbouring authority], would undoubtedly have been in special schools. Proportionally they have two and a half times the number of children in special schools that we have.'

Sadly, there was a belief that primary and secondary, but particularly secondary, schools are ill-prepared to cope with children with special educational needs, particularly those who had already been taken from the ordinary system precisely because they were failing to thrive in that sector. Although these professionals could be accused of being overprotective, the reality was that most seemed keen to retain some segregated places as refuges for those children who found themselves in schools that were unfit or unable to cater for the child's needs. It seems a sad indictment of our system if special schools will always be required, but it is certainly clear that educational psychologists and advisers are not without their qualms about the idea of total integration, and despite some criticisms of the special school curriculum, which was accused of being too narrow and limited in some schools, special schools were seen as being appropriate environments for some children. A psychologist said: 'I think you've got to recognize that special schools are good for some children. I accept that they're not good for all children and that many children ending up in special schools ought not to have ended up in special schools and have suffered from being in special schools. But some children haven't and one thing which ought to be looked at is which children do in fact benefit from being in special schools, the provision of special schools, because some children do.'

At best, special schools were seen as fulfilling not only educational but also emotional needs. One psychologist said: 'It's quite nice. Some youngsters undoubtedly do go in and blossom because they're as good as everybody else and they've never been as good as everybody else in their whole lives and you do see some youngsters positively bloom.' Another argued: 'There are lots of kids in ESN-M schools who are more competent than some kids in ordinary schools. They are that way because of the help they are getting and the growth in their self-esteem.'

SUMMARY

Awareness of the constraints outlined above left psychologists and advisers in agreement with the principle of integration but fearful of the reality. There was a considerable degree of dissatisfaction with primary and secondary schools as they stood, which was to do not only with resources but also with curriculum, teacher skills and attitudes. Some feared that to incorporate children with greater educational needs than those of children already in the system would be to increase the problems of schools while simultaneously failing to meet the educational and emotional needs of some children. One principal educational psychologist summed up this view as follows '[Integration] must be adequately funded and adequately serviced. And I'm worried that, if you look at the growth of separate special education, it grew out of the philosophy that normal schools couldn't cope with what they were getting. And to reverse the process overnight without any careful planning would be a nonsense in my opinion. We'd just be adding to the problems of schools that are not really coping very well with the ordinary range of kids that they've got. I think we're failing a lot of kids in our education. Despite all the money that's spent, we're not doing a very good job. I think in many ways, for in some schools 50 per cent or even 60 per cent of the population in the education system, that it's inappropriate.'

Chapter 2

The Statement: Possibilities and Constraints

POSSIBILITIES

The Warnock Report, the 1981 Education Act and the circulars that followed it all indicated that the statement was to be maintained on a small proportion of the school population. The Warnock Report did not envisage that it would be necessary for a child to be assessed by a multi-professional team if his or her needs could be met by the ordinary school's resources, even if these were 'supplemented when necessary by, say, the part-time services of an additional teacher'. The point was that they were resources that were 'readily available to or within the ordinary school' (Warnock, 1978, 4:39). The 1981 Education Act reflected this stance, although some doubt remained over exactly what constituted provision that was 'additional to, or otherwise different from' that generally made (1:3a). It was an issue picked up and elaborated on by Circular 1/83 (DES and DHSS, 1983). Formal procedures were unnecessary where the resources for special educational provision came under the canopy of those provided by the ordinary school, and this applied whether the child was receiving tuition within the school or attending a reading centre. Nor were they required where provision was expected to be of a short duration.

Even with this description of what did *not* constitute an extra resource the situation remained unclear, because what constituted an extra resource in one school could be part of the school's existing resources in another. The Act made no direct reference to this crucial point, although it was briefly noted in paragraph 14 of Circular 1/83, where it served as an explanation of why greater clarity could not be proffered in defining what constituted an 'additional or otherwise different' resource: 'The deciding factors in determining what constitutes additional or otherwise different provision are likely to vary from area to area depending on the range of provision normally available in an authority's school.' A child, it seemed, could be educated without a statement in one school because resources were available and deployed in such a way as to enable staff to cater for that child, while in another a child with the equivalent difficulties, in terms of nature and degree, would require a statement.

In the acknowledgement of this lay the promise of a radical change in practice.

Although the Act, like the Warnock Report, intended the statement to be used sparingly, there was nothing to suggest that the provision of a statement should result in the exclusion of the child from the ordinary school. On the contrary, the wording of paragraph 14 of Circular 1/83 evokes the image of the statement as a document that will bring resources into the ordinary school: 'As a general rule, the Secretary of State expects LEAs to afford the protection of a statement to all children who have severe or complex learning difficulties which require the provision of extra resources in ordinary schools.'

The Act might, therefore, have been seen as something that promised to level out inequalities in provision. The associated circulars acknowledged that provision for children with special educational needs varied from one school to another, while leaving open the possibility that the child with a statement could be educated at primary or secondary school. Although one child might have a statement and another with the equivalent difficulties might not, it was at last becoming feasible that both might receive the resources they required to enable them to cope within the ordinary school system. Theoretically at least, the way was open for steps to be taken towards creating equal educational opportunities for children with special educational needs.

The Act recognizes that placements cannot be made independent of resource considerations. The placement of a child in an ordinary school must be compatible with 'the efficient use of resources' (1981 Education Act, 2:3c), so placements will invariably be subject to financial constraints. It is the possible merging of children's interests and financial interests that is particularly disconcerting. One psychologist, describing administration as a 'prime area for both financial and political pressure', argued strongly against the merger. Before the Act actions planned for a child by the professionals involved had been subject to the administrator's intervention if they had not been expedient in political or financial terms, but all concerned had been clear about why the decision was changed. 'If there were any changes to be made it was all seen as being the administrator stepping in and saying, "I'm sorry but the financial and administrative aspects of this are such that I'm going to change it". It was all obviously clear: "That might be the right decision from the point of view of the child, but it's not expedient from our point of view, for it to happen".' Ultimately, therefore, the authority may know what is best but choose to take a different line.

The effect of this situation on those who are regularly asked to submit advice may be a debilitating one. For example, an educational psychologist's awareness of the authority's limitations, in terms of resources and professional experience which enables him or her to predict what provision might realistically be made for the child, makes it nonsensical to write elaborate advice offering imaginative variations on how the child's needs might be best met. There would be little point in recommending facilities and resources that did not exist. The psychologist is thus caught between making recommendations for facilities and resources to meet the child's needs and the administrator's red pen. One way out of this difficulty is to write advice with resource constraints in mind. Despite the fact that the DES and DHSS Circular 1/83 stipulates that this should not be the case, it seems that this is what some educational psychologists do. Indeed, to do otherwise would be to produce outlandish resource recommendations that administrators, who have their own financial pressures to contend with, could only fail to put into practice. In some authorities it would seem that statements are not, after all, a means of ensuring that children's needs are met. As one psychologist explained,

'There are no new resources and so some of the statements are fairly thin. We're not using it at present as a way of ensuring that children's needs are met.' Perhaps because of the practical financial constraints on the statement, the advantages were portrayed by those interviewed in more general terms, such as increasing awareness and providing a degree of protection for the child.

The protection provided by the statement was raised by most interviewees, even though its operation and definition varied. The statement could, for example, protect the child via a definition of needs and the requirement for regular reviews. This would enable easier monitoring of individual, and groups of, children in relation to a process and its effects. Where a method seemed unsatisfactory or inappropriate, steps could be taken to alter the situation. Yet it seemed that not all authorities were using this aspect of the statement to full advantage. While it was clear that some administrators had taken on the role of monitor, the role remained unfilled in other authorities.

Another particularly important way in which the statement was seen as being advantageous to the child lay in its legal nature. Where resources, of whatever type, were committed they had to remain committed unless there was a change in the child's needs. Thus an authority that sought to change its policy and, for example, cut back on support services for children with special educational needs in ordinary schools would find it very difficult to do so if provision was written into their final statements. This was a common interpretation of the statement's value. As one psychologist argued: 'I should think everybody shares the same philosophy that on the whole a statement will offer an additional useful purpose as a safeguard against some kind of eventuality of changing policy if, for any reason, the policy of the region did change and economies were looked for in the area of special education.'

Several psychologists identified a further benefit in the statement: that it was specifically geared to meeting the needs of the child, which were, they pointed out, not always reflected in the wishes of the child's parents. For example, in cases where parents could not, or would not, accept that their child had special educational needs which the authority felt were such as to require them 'to determine the special educational provision that should be made for him' (1981 Education Act, 5:1), they were empowered by the Act to assess them formally and, if necessary, to prepare a statement. Although the LEA must take into account any representations made by parents it is not compelled to agree with them (1981 Education Act, 5:5 and 8). Similarly, when the statement is prepared an appeal committee may 'confirm the special educational provision specified in the statement', as may the Secretary of State (1981 Education Act, 8:4 and 8:7). As the DES and DHSS Circular points out, 'the ultimate responsibility for assessing the child's special educational needs rests with the LEA' (Circular 1/83, IV:39).

Generally, the fact that the statement was formed not only from the views of professionals but also from those of the child's parents was an advantage identified in the majority of authorities. Parents' wishes usually coincided with the needs of their child and when this was the case it was possible for them to act through the statement to promote their child's interests. It is clear that their representations and appeals could be overruled and that they might not get the provision they wanted, but they had at least been provided with a system that enabled them to fight if they so wished. Formal opportunities had been provided for them to intervene and in this sense the statement protected their rights. Although many authorities stressed that they had involved parents in the decision-making process before the 1981 Education Act, it was welcomed as a statutory requirement: 'I like the idea of parents being involved as of right rather than in practice.' It was a code of practice that all authorities, whatever their previous practice, had to follow.

It must be concluded that the prevailing attitude to the advantages of the statement was ambivalent, particularly among psychologists. All were able to identify some advantages, but the majority of these were accompanied by qualifications. These indicated that the advantages would only emerge if conditions were conducive to them doing so, and that the current climate was certainly not seen as one likely to enhance them. While the statement was, as one psychologist said, 'potentially tremendous', it was impossible to use it as 'a means of ensuring that children's needs are met' because the resources were not available to do so. Unless these were provided many advantages would continue to lie unrealized.

CONSTRAINTS ON RESOURCES

Limited resources meant that theory could not be translated into practice, and in only two of the seventeen authorities was the statement described as being beneficial to the child by obliging the authority to commit resources. In the remaining LEAs there was a reluctance to assess formally and prepare a statement in the first instance, and a reluctance to provide resources even if it was prepared.

At the early stage after the Act, considerable care was being taken not to set precedents that authorities felt they might not be able to maintain. One psychologist explained how in his own authority children in need of a small amount of special help that did not fall within the school's resources were not provided with statements or any extra help: 'A normally intelligent child, average or above, whose basic skills are still poor. If you write a statement that says that child needs a phonic programme to develop reading and spelling and the secondary school says, "we cannot meet this need, we are not staffed to meet this need, we can't afford to allocate this amount of capitation to buying staffing and equipment resources", then it's really very difficult. Now the authority in that sort of situation is choosing not to write statements. They are saying, "we will make the schools aware of the child's needs, but we won't actually grasp that nettle". I regret that.'

In another authority instructions had been received from the administration to recommend for assessment only those children whom they felt would require separate special educational provision. The principal educational psychologist explained: 'The guidance we've had from the boss so far, indirectly, is "only put names forward if you're fairly sure the child will need segregated special education".' He believed such guidance came from the director's 'genuine desire to be administratively swift and clear'. There were no resources available that could be directed into ordinary schools, so any child who needed extra resources had to be placed in separate special education. The indirect guidance served to protect the interests of those 'marginal' children who needed extra help but whose needs were not severe enough to warrant placement in separate special provision. Unless assessment was thought about carefully before being proposed a child they hoped would be granted extra resources in an ordinary school could well end up in separate provision. The director was said to view the situation in clear, practical terms:

'The director's saying "What does this mean in practice? Leaving all subleties aside what it means in practice is that this child will require extra teaching resources. Normally my budgetary demands are such that the only way I'm going to be able to make these available is by putting the child in segregated special education. So, boys and girls, think very carefully before putting a name forward for formal assessment. Do you really want this child in segregated special education?"'

This practice not only has little grounding in law but also seems unlikely to result in a good match between children's needs and appropriate provision, and not all were happy with the director's stance. Educational psychologists were not only criticizing the approach but were also refusing to adhere to it. The principal educational psychologist explained: 'We're standing out against this and saying, "we'd like to adopt a philosophy whereby we put names forward where we think the child will require extra resources, whatever they may be". Most educational psychologists are operating a criterion something like, "I am not prepared to say that this child does not now or will not in the future need extra resources whether they be teaching—an extra teacher specifically employed for the purpose—or not, now or at some stage in the future", and we're not prepared to go along with this idea that statementing means segregated special education. In our view that's not what the Act's about.'

This latter argument reflected the second problem, which is that where children did have statements prepared on them the chances were that the statement would recommend special school or unit placement. The reality was that for the child unlucky enough to be attending the primary or secondary school lacking in resources to cater for his or her special educational needs, it was far more likely that he or she would be assessed and placed in a special school or unit than that resources would be allocated to the environment the child was already in. There were few children with statements being educated in ordinary primary and secondary school classrooms. The comment 'it is much more difficult to get a child statemented in an ordinary school because it has resource implications' was reiterated in all authorities. 'This authority', said one principal educational psychologist, 'hasn't really come to terms with this issue of the statement of needs being a statement of resources.'

This stance frustrated many psychologists. The conflict lay between the ideal and the constraint; the knowledge that with extra help in the ordinary school a child could cope grinding against an awareness that the authority was unable to commit resources in this way. One reported: 'I went to see a child in the ordinary school the other day ... and I'm recommending, with some degree of hesitancy, placing a child in a special school where I feel that if we had the resources, that child might be maintained in the ordinary school.'

Unable to provide the child with the necessary resources in an ordinary school classroom, the psychologist must assess the risk involved if the child is left without such support. One, considering the likelihood of a special attachment teacher being provided for a child in an ordinary school, commented: 'I think if it was going to be actually implemented it would have to form part of the child's statement otherwise there'd be no guarantee of it. Now whether the authority would commit itself in that way I just don't know. It would depend on whether they feel they've got the resources and at the moment there's not much sign of resources being made available, there's been no additional resources made available.'

Children with special educational needs who were retained or placed in ordinary schools with statements tended to be those with physical disabilities who, with the necessary resources, were academically and socially capable of coping in ordinary schools. Resources here generally referred to a particular piece of equipment. Instances of a teacher being attached to a child were far less common and in some authorities it seemed that the switch in resource requirement, from the need for a piece of equipment to the need for a support teacher, constituted a cut-off point. 'If we had a child with special needs [who needs equipment], that child goes right to the top of the list for admission to that school under the protection of the statement and we would supply things like hearing aids, anything they needed.' Children in this authority who had some other physical disability might also be placed in an ordinary school: 'We've had blind children in our comprehensives, not in that particular school, but in other schools where, because of the choice of syllabus, it's been a better place for them to go.'

In other authorities other criteria applied: 'I would think that the children in our mainstream who get statemented at the moment, and the ones who are in the pipeline, are children who have a multiplicity of difficulties, but when you weigh everything in the balance they can hold their own in mainstream.' The adviser gave an example of one such child: 'We've got one child who's a severe sight loss and I don't think he's really spastic, but he's obviously got some kind of brain damage that's caused him to have physical problems, and he's holding his own in mainstream but obviously he's a statemented child. He's as bright as a button and he's been held back very severely because of some of his physical problems. On one side he's very damaged and can't do things like his buttons and zips and so on.'

Another group of children with statements were the children of parents who had pressed their authority for a statement. Many in this group were deemed dyslexic and some were children whom their authority would probably not have chosen to prepare statements on. However, when parents were insistent the authority tended to oblige. As one principal educational psychologist explained: 'There's one or two we would probably choose not to hold a statement on as an authority, but it's felt that as parents are insisting and they want it, we are prepared to make a statement which will specify what we think the child requires.'

To summarize, the statement, in its conception, was intended for a small group of children with severe educational needs and these were indeed the children on whom statements were being prepared. However, what does not seem to have been intended was that the statement should be strictly synonymous with separate special school or unit provision. With the advice collated and the statement drafted, often by one person, there was a potential to bring a greater degree of equality to the quality of provision made for children with special educational needs within an authority. At the time the study was conducted it was clear that this was not the case. A lack of resources was prohibiting change, and it seemed that more often than not statements had been sucked into and adapted to pre-1983 practice. All too often the statement was found to be synonymous with separate special school or unit provision. That it was able to be used in this way lends support to the view of some professionals that the 1981 Education Act was not a vehicle of integration.

CONSTRAINTS ON PROCEDURES

The provision of advice

Major constraints on the effectiveness of the delivery system were connected with assessment and the production of the statement, although these were obviously also affected by resource constraints, particularly in terms of the need for increased manpower. The central problem seemed to be the pragmatic one of actually getting the statement produced within what each authority saw as being a reasonable length of time, a problem exacerbated by requirements of the Act, and by the process of acquiring the necessary advice.

The 1981 Education Act brought with it three major changes affecting the production of a report. First, the SE forms were withdrawn and an explicit distinction was made between

   (i)   the analysis of the child's learning difficulties;
   (ii) the specification of his special needs for different kinds of approaches, facilities and resources;
  (iii) the determination of the special educational provision to meet these needs.

(DES and DHSS, 1983, II:4)

which was to be reflected in advice presented (IV:23). Secondly, reports were to be open. Advice was to be attached to the statement and the statement forwarded to parents. There had been no such routine distribution of professional reports before. Thirdly, in many authorities the responsibility for making the decision concerning provision changed from one group of professionals, usually educational psychologists, to another, administrators. This meant that in addition to reports being open to parents they were also open to the scrutiny of a wide audience of professionals and clerical staff.

Confidentiality thereby became an issue which affected some professional groups more than others. For example, the writing of advice for a statement was incompatible with the need of medical officers to protect the right of confidentiality. They were said to be dealing with this situation by responding briefly to requests for advice, on the basis that the less said, the less could be revealed. One principal educational psychologist thought the situation was about to deteriorate further and that medics would be reluctant to submit any advice at all: 'It hasn't hit us yet but I can see it's not very far off happening. There's something from the BMA to the effect that doctors must not breach their patients' rights of confidentiality on pain of being struck off and we're likely to find that doctors are going to be in a very difficult position in providing advice to an authority on a child.... Where general practitioners are actually the ones to provide advice ... they're going to be much less inclined to engage in a game of shuffling reports around goodness knows what administrative officer, they're only interested in patient welfare.... Some authorities are running into a brick wall on the medical side.'

Consultant psychiatrists were said to be similarly reluctant to write advice for statements. Because they viewed their relationships with each other, the child and the child's parents as being highly confidential, the prospect of committing their thoughts to paper and producing a report that might be read by a large number of people was not favourably perceived.

The medical officers' difficulties did not only centre on the issue of confidentiality. In some authorities they were also said to have too much to do. Inevitably this meant that the amount of time they could spend on each statement was very limited. They were forced to redefine the task into one they could cope with. While this meant that their reports were perhaps of a poorer quality, there was no other strategy they could adopt that would not create further delays in an already slow, delay-ridden system. As one psychologist commented: 'I'm sure our medics don't do anything like the amount of work that they're supposed to do under the Act because they can't cope with the workload.'

In another authority the way in which one medical officer, whose task was to cover all reassessments, had handled her work was described: 'Where reassessments are concerned there's one SMO [senior medical officer] doing the lot, which she just can't cope with. It's too much, so she's giving basic information.'

To cut back on labour this senior medical officer and her colleagues had devised a standard advice form: 'They've devised a form—they just type the answers in and usually it's just a few lines.' In another authority the situation was summed up as follows: 'I think they're a little worried about the medical reporting. They're certainly under a lot of pressure, there aren't enough so they're having to do them quickly and they don't have much time for writing them up. They're certainly worried about the confidentiality issue. That's been their response, a standard, quickly filled in, single sheet of paper.'

Concern about confidentiality was also expressed regarding parents who were not seen to act in accordance with their child's interests, as in child abuse cases. Here some professionals found it difficult to write freely and unreservedly as an advocate for the child. Thus although the Act was referred to by the Advisory Centre for Education as a 'parent's charter', it could, as one principal educational psychologist pointed out, fail to be a charter for children: 'There are some children where being an advocate for the parent means you need a different person to be an advocate for the child, and I think the Act hasn't realized that.' In such circumstances professionals opted not to include the information, in order to protect the child: 'There are some pupils where if you write honestly what you know or are aware of, factual information about the child's home circumstances, and it's going to go through the documents and the process of the Act, then there are things which you would need to say to protect the child that you couldn't possibly put in a report.'

In one authority a strategy had been adopted to remove the advice writer's dilemma. Highly confidential information was presented in a report available only to professionals. 'The difficulty has come where it's known that the child might be put at risk or the welfare of the family be put at risk if information is disclosed in a casual manner. I'm referring particularly to non-accidental injury cases or cases of a condition which is either temporary or private. I mean things like marital difficulties or rent arrears might be highly pertinent to a child's problems but not appropriate to put down in a broadcast form which will be seen by large numbers of people. For that reason we have followed guidance from the medical officer of the DHSS, who advised the DES that, not exactly a two-tier system of reporting, but we would follow the guidance of the Act which says the authority seeks advice so the psychologists will do their professional report which will be seen by professional people dealing with the child, and they will also submit their advice on a separate sheet of paper, and *that* advice will be open for the parents to see or any other professionals to see. The medical authority does likewise. We've asked social services to do likewise and in some cases social workers do that, otherwise they send their full report.'

Another tactic was to withhold information which was felt to be confidential or likely to offend parents, but this ran the risk of producing a report that would be so diluted and neutral that it would be of little help to the compiler of the statement. For other advice writers (schoolteachers, social workers, education psychologists and nurses, for example) the need to impart critical information that might be interpreted by parents as being offensive was seen as being at best challenging and at worst very difficult.

Although some psychologists suggested that they were highly experienced in communicating delicate information in a written form, all acknowledged the difficulty of writing in an objective, non-judgemental manner. This was a difficulty they, along with other professionals, had wrestled with. Although complaints from parents about the content of reports were said to be few, those written by educational welfare officers, social workers and teachers were apt to cause some contention. And despite acknowledging that reports received from professionals within groups varied tremendously, many principal educational psychologists went on to criticize severely the very poor quality of the weaker ones.

School reports came in for the greatest criticism. It was claimed that they were apt to include unsubstantiated comments that parents reacted vehemently to: 'There've been one or two problems with the schools. I mean they've put in things that parents have objected to because it's totally unsubstantiated, sort of rumour and things like that. Parents have hit the roof.' Stressing the need for consciousness of the legal implications of report-writing one psychologist said: 'I think it's very salutary for anybody who writes a report on a child to bear in mind that you may be called upon to defend your comments in the report in a legal setting.' It seemed that some teachers were neglecting to bear this in mind.

Advice from schools was also criticized on the grounds that it failed to go into sufficient detail about the child's needs and how those needs might be met. It was stated coldly that on some teachers' reports there were 'a lot of blank spaces', and reports were described as focusing on 'getting rid of the child'. In an effort to control quality some principal educational psychologists had assumed the task of checking advice from schools. One objected to this strongly on the grounds that it was unprofessional. Teachers should, he felt, be able to express their own educational views about children: 'At the moment I'm frankly disgusted at the very poor quality of remarks and observations about kids.... Some of my colleagues in other authorities felt that they should check, but I'm sorry, that's unprofessional. If a teacher can't put his own views down in a proper way, it just reflects badly on that teacher.' One adviser said that teachers had particular difficulties with the final section of the report. After specifying the child's needs they were uncertain how to proceed. The task was now more demanding. Previously they had simply named a school, now they had to specify the type of help required without citing a particular institution: 'The difficulty is really one of tradition. In the past they've always said, "The child needs the sort of regime he can get in", and then named a school. Now they are being asked not to name a school but to say what sort of help they need. One or two of them are having difficulty with this.'

A further problem identified was the use of jargon. Open reports were not really fully open if the language they were written in was not accessible to all readers, but many professionals were having difficulties in this area. A recent incident was cited as an example of the gap between terms used by an advice writer and the parent's comprehension: 'The last mother I saw I went through the bumph with her. "Do you understand this? Do you understand this?" Came to the speech therapist's report and it talked about expressive language and dyspraxia and stuff like that she obviously wouldn't know. "Do you know what we can do about that?" "No". So I had to interpret that. Well, I think that's wrong really. I think we'll have to have a meeting and talk about it. But all the professionals are trained to use big words and suddenly you can't. It's jolly difficult.' To write and communicate meaning exactly without using jargon was acknowledged as being a real skill. It was also recognized that unless this skill was acquired by professionals the content of reports would remain obscure to many parents, defeating the object of having open reports.

Members of all professions were said to be experiencing difficulties in focusing their attention solely on the child's needs in the early stages of the procedures, without giving consideration to possible provision. In addition some had difficulty in restricting their written observations to their own professional spheres. Failing to adhere to the stipulations of Circular 1/83, they tended to comment on areas in which they had no professional training. The following is a comment typical of that made in a number of authorities: 'Some professionals have difficulty in being precise about what is really needed in terms of their own expertise and separating that expertise from that other professionals are best able to give.' The main culprits in this sense were said to be the doctors, who frequently encroached on the educationalists' territory.

When the cause of difficulties and resultant weaknesses in professional advice was identified as being among those that generated dilemmas for all professionals the response was sympathetic. However, when advice was seen as being unjustifiably poor, as in the case of some pre-school and school advice, the criticism was harsh and led to many arguing that teacher training at both initial and in-service levels should include training in report writing: 'I think they need to look very carefully at teacher education. It sounds patronizing but I'm still going to make the statement that teachers aren't always the best at producing coherent reports. I think there's a fair amount of in-service work required.'

Alongside this clear call for training in writing advice for teachers, some professionals said that they would like to see much greater guidance being given to parents. Parents were conspicuous among contributors to the statement in that they, unlike essential contributors, had not been provided with any guidance from central government on how they might structure their representations. Although in some authorities it was evident that considerable help was given, this was not always the case. Not surprisingly, in those latter authorities there were calls for improvements.

Delays in advice provision

Demands in the legislation itself exacerbated the delays in the system. For example, the waiting periods for parents to make representations were described as being 'in-built delays'. The 29-day period following the serving of the notice of the intention to assess (1981 Education Act, 5:3) was singled out for particular criticism, being generally condemned as 'time-wasting'. It was appreciated that parents had been provided with formal opportunities to intervene in the process, but where it was known that parents were in agreement with the authority's proposal, the period was seen as being futile and confusing for parents. One principal educational psychologist outlined the scenario: 'You write to the office recommending something that the parents are in total agreement with, wait till they [the parents] get a letter through the post saying "is it all right if we go ahead with formal assessment?", wait another month for the letter that's written by the parent to come back to you with a request for formal assessment, and quite often they'll ring you up and say, "but we've already said we'll go ahead with it, what's it all about?". And you start to explain to them, "I'm afraid that although I've spoken to you at great length and although I've been into the school and seen your child working in the classroom, etc., and I've spoken to everybody concerned and I think we are probably going to have to make some special provision, you still have to write to the office saying, 'I recommend that you should institute formal procedures'."'

Not all authorities chose to wait for the 29-day period to be exhausted before taking action. One education officer said that although the 'strict legal advice' was to wait, when parents replied quickly indicating that they wanted the authority to go ahead with assessment, the authority did so immediately.

The need to take into account advice from all sources, as specified in the Education (Special Educational Needs) Regulations (DES 1983, 29:8), had also slowed down the process. Representations and evidence from parents were to be given full consideration, and advice from the educational psychologist, the medical officer, the school and any other sources the authority considered it important to include had to be submitted before the statement could be compiled. However, while parents were given 29 days in which to submit their evidence, no such time limit was placed on professionals. As copies of all advice had to be appended to the statement (DES and DHSS, 1983, IV:42), it is clear that for authorities to operate on anything less than all the advice could prove a risky action for them to take. It is evident that a delay in professional advice resulted in a delay in the whole process. This presented a new situation, since delays in the submission of reports in the past had not necessarily halted the procedures. An education officer explained: 'The main criterion previously was the SE3, the educational psychologist's report, and you could proceed on that—I mean technically you shouldn't but you could proceed on that. You can't do that anymore because you have to have the medical advice and the educational advice to let parents see before you proceed.'

Medical advice was singled out as being most likely to be delayed, with the comment, 'we've always had problems with medical advice', being made in a number of authorities. It was not a new problem, but was exacerbated by the Act. Authorities could no longer respond by taking action without the report. They simply had to wait.

There were other causes of delays in advice submission that were direct consequences of the legislation. Some psychologists said they were now less able to produce their own advice promptly. One reason they offered for this was that the reports now had to be more detailed. 'The reports are rather more complex now, rather more difficult to compose. Whereas previously one could identify what the child's difficulties were and recommended a particular course of action, now we have to identify what the child's difficulties are and come up with at least the backbone of a programme of curricular action.' A second was rooted in advice being presented with the statement for parents to examine. Advice had to be accurate, objective and inoffensive and some found that this required them to be more circumspect, with the consequence being that such reports took longer to compose.

The problem with delays was not simply the obvious one that children's special educational needs were not promptly catered for. A prime difficulty was that delays often created or aggravated parental anxiety. One principal educational psychologist, who accused the procedure of taking 'a totally unreasonable length of time from the point of referral to actually getting a child the right kind of help', drew on a recent incident to illustrate the distress caused to parents. 'I've had a parent on the phone this morning for a considerable length of time extremely distressed that it has taken in effect three months from the date that I saw the child to the point when all the advice is now lying at the desk of the officer who has to make the decision of placement. The parent is not interested in the ins and outs of the curricular advice. She is only interested in "Where is my little girl going?".'

Parents found delays both upsetting and annoying, particularly when a professional contravened Circular 1/83 (IV:35) and told parents early in the procedure that, for example, a placement at a particular school would be better for their child. Because they interpreted this as a decision taken, the delay that followed seemed inexplicable to the parents, who were then apt to argue: 'Well, you knew three months ago what he needed. Why are you taking all this time to get round to making a decision?'

In this sense, informing parents from the outset of exactly what was happening administratively, without being able to inform them about what provision would be made for their child, was unhelpful. Before the implementation of the Act delays had not caused much anger for two reasons: first, because parents were often informed at an early stage in the proceedings what provision would be made for their child; and secondly, because it was not unusual for them to be completely unaware that reports were being prepared. One principal educational psychologist explained: 'In the old days under the SE system parents didn't know what was going on. There was often just as long a delay, I think, in the processing of papers and writing of things and so on, but parents didn't know that they were going to get anything on paper. It was all a secret.'

There is clearly a need to minimize the length of time between referral and placement. Many felt that the procedures could be streamlined, and that their own cautiousness in dealing with the Act during its first years of operation was a contributory factor. They had been anxious not to contravene the law and had followed the regulations closely. Their hope was that experience in working with the Act would enable them to take time-saving measures. The comment of one adviser for special education was typical: 'We are beginning to take short-cuts in certain areas where we feel we can speed the thing up.'

It was not always clear that such modifications would really be effective in lessening the time it took to conduct the procedures. In one authority, for example, requests for advice from professionals had been sent out sequentially, as suggested in DES and DHSS Circular 1/83 (IV:32). Finding this method protracted they planned to speed up the process by sending out their requests simultaneously. However, this system too had problems. Professionals were without the advice of others when entering a case, and at times this meant they had little information about children before seeing them. 'Going in cold', as one principal educational psychologist referred to it, lengthened the procedure because they had to spend time finding out the basics of the case. Another thought that the process would be streamlined to such an extent that it would simply correspond with pre-1983 practice: 'I guess people will write their advice in a triter manner. It'll be reduced back to the previous system where a decision is made, everybody agrees with it and you're just doing the paperwork to legalize the decision. In essence that's what happens to probably 75–80 per cent of the problems.... People know what's what and this is just an administrative procedure tacked on the end.'

In some authorities the effects of delays caused by the Act were particularly severe. In one of these, where no modifications had been made to practice at the time of interviewing, 'wholesale changes' were predicted by a senior psychologist. He saw these as being both inevitable and essential. In his opinion the authority's procedures were in danger of breaking down completely. It was taking a long time for children to be placed and their assessment units were 'choked up' with children waiting for their statements to be completed so that they could move into alternative provision. The authority was attempting to adhere to the statute, so that children's needs had to be fully assessed and the statement completed before they were placed in long-term provision. While acknowledging the authority's views as honourable, the senior psychologist was concerned that the consequences for children were negative. Other authorities, he suggested, were choosing to operate differently, in a way he felt was to the child's advantage: 'I know some authorities are being ... different and in my view they are breaking the law in the interests of children.' It was crucial, he felt, that a greater degree of flexibility was introduced to practice in his own authority.

The increased formality of the procedures and the greater length of time it took for them to be accomplished were the two major factors identified as impeding the efficient functioning of the procedures. There was also concern about relationships with parents. Professionals were obliged to operate within a legal framework and careless talk could cause future difficulties. These influences were accused of exerting an inhibitory effect on informal discussions, as an adviser explained: 'Once we start statementing we are in a kind of legal partnership with parents and we have to act according to procedures, and that's removed the ability, particularly for [the principal educational psychologist], to have informal on-going discussions with parents as we used to.' Enforced reticence imposed stress on relationships that had previously been open, and also on some professionals who had been obliged to modify their approach. In view of these considerations it was perhaps inevitable that one principal educational psychologist should draw an analogy between the legal framework and a strait-jacket.

Clearly, an adviser's inability to reassure parents about where their child would be placed was potentially a very upsetting experience, and in some circumstances it was evident that educational psychologists were unwilling to adhere to the stipulation. One said simply: 'We tend to break the rules a bit. If parents are insistent we can give them options. "It could be that if you're asking me for my opinion, my opinion is that the child would be better off ... , but I'm not supposed to say that because I'm not supposed to commit the authority to anything".'

Overall, one of the most powerful arguments presented was that the procedures and the manner in which they were executed raised parental expectations well beyond what the authority was actually able to provide. The very bureaucracy of the procedures had caused some parents to assume that they would lead to 'something marvellous' being produced for their child, while the reality was that limited financial resources prevented this.

A further dimension of the procedures which was said to be anxiety-provoking was the written material forwarded to parents; this tended to be overly formal and bureaucratic. Providing parents with a readily intelligible explanation of the effect of the procedures from sections 4–7, covering the identification, assessment and statement of children's special educational needs, was particularly difficult. Despite the difficulty an explanation had, by law, to be provided. 'Before making such a statement a local authority shall serve on the parent of the child concerned ... a written explanation of the effect of subsections (4) to (7) below' (Education Act, 1981, 7:3).

Unfortunately the written product tended to be unintelligible and intimidating. One education officer said, 'To many parents [it] reads like gobbledygook', and advocated that those responsible for this directive should also be responsible for producing an explanation for parents: 'While there is a duty within the Act upon the authority to tell parents of the practical effects of subsections 4–7, people who have drafted that by way of legislation should have the task of conveying the effect of that to parents.' Although he had given the task of producing a comprehensible explanation to various groups of people, none had accomplished it. 'I've given that task to groups of people and I've yet to see something which is readily intelligible even to informed and thinking people. It's a very difficult task.'

If the consequences of the formality and complexity of the procedures ended only with professionals having to tax themselves to produce comprehensible material for parents, the problem would appear to be a manageable, if very difficult, one. However, it was apparent that this merely constituted part of the problem. Those who had responsibility to write the draft or final statement had a special complaint. Pointing to piles of papers, one principal educational psychologist said: 'Just as you see, we've got piles of the damn things to do! They're all around the room. We're just coping with the paperwork, quite frankly.' Even those who were not directly involved in writing advice or statements expressed sympathy with those who were. The procedure was notorious: 'I'm not involved in the procedure, no. I've nothing but sympathy for the people who are. I think they're cumbersome.'

Writing and explaining the procedures and their effects was draining professional time to the extent that many psychologists were dissatisfied with their practice. They had less time to spend on preventative work and felt that schools were getting a 'poorer deal' than they had before the Act. Many thought it ironical that they were spending an increased proportion of their time on children who required resources beyond those offered by the ordinary school, and less time on work that might prevent those needs arising. It was a source of much professional frustration. The unavailability of psychologists, coupled with the delays in providing for children, was a growing source of discontentment in schools. 'The ordinary schools are complaining more and more bitterly on the one hand that their educational psychologists no longer come because they haven't got the time, and on the other hand that it's taking ages to get children placed.'

Giving full consideration to parents' wishes and discussing issues with them fully, factors indicating the incorporation of parents into the decision-making body, were seen ambivalently by education officers, although many expressed a willingness to provide the time necessary for discussion with parents. They acknowledged that time spent in the early stages of the procedures could prevent an appeal being lodged later, but were conscious that such discussions were exceedingly time-consuming. 'Time' was a word that was automatically included in reference to discussion with parents, and it was this awareness of the demand the process made on time that led one adviser to describe it as 'an expensive luxury'.

Nevertheless, through all the descriptions of the attendant difficulties of the statement ran optimism that the procedures would be more swiftly operated as professionals became more experienced in implementing them and, in some cases, that the procedures would be modified. Certainly, if they were not modified on a national level, some authorities would be obliged to modify them locally in order to operate. Moreover, not all those who saw the procedures as being over-elaborate condemned them. Some accepted them as being a price that had to be paid. One adviser commented: 'I think if you believe in children's rights, parental involvement and open accountability that's one of the prices we have to pay. I think I'd still rather have it than not have it. I wouldn't like to go back to the SE procedures.'

The idea of a statement commended itself to many of those interviewed. As one educational psychologist pointed out: 'I think the idea that ultimately a child has a statement of its needs and appropriate provision ... bound in with a set of reports is super, really excellent.' This sentiment was echoed by another, who said that 'every disadvantage I think, on the whole, would be counterbalanced, more than counterbalanced, by an advantage'. In short, professionals found no quarrel with the principles underlying the statement. The criticisms lay in its production and, although many of the potential advantages it proffered could not be realized because of financial restrictions, the idea of a statement was widely supported.

A similar degree of support was found for the concept of integration. No one disagreed with the principle. As one adviser declared: 'I haven't met anybody, I haven't met a special school teacher, an administrator, an adviser, a psychologist or anybody working in this authority who wouldn't want it [integration].' However, what was emphasized was the gulf many saw between the idea and the reality. They were convinced that, unless major changes took place in primary and secondary schools, to practise a policy of integration which involved a dramatic reduction in the numbers of special school places available would be to penalize some children with special educational needs. It is to practice that we now turn by examining the integration of five children into secondary schools.

Chapter 3

The Integration Process.
I: The Children and Their School Histories

Before the process of integration for each of the five children is described some background information must be given, in particular on how they found themselves in special schools in the first place.

JONATHAN

Jonathan was first referred to the schools psychological service for 'slow progress' at the age of 6. He had, to use the head teacher's phrase, 'been integrated' there until his sixth birthday and had then been transferred into a remedial class of ten junior and two infant children. This placement was not successful because, in the view of the school, he needed much individual attention. At the time of referral Jonathan was described by the head teacher as leading a solitary existence, enjoying 'solitary occupations which require little intelligence', such as brick building. Nevertheless, the other children appeared to 'tolerate him in a kindly way'.

Jonathan was assessed by an educational psychologist at the age of 6.8. His verbal quotient on the WISC-R was 65, as was his performance quotient. He was described in the report as 'quiet, undemonstrative but co-operative', and as being of low ability, lacking in confidence and preferring to isolate himself. The report concluded that 'Jonathan is a pleasant, polite boy of low general intellectual ability. His perceptual, linguistic and associative skills are uniformly weak and it is unlikely that he will make progress in the normal school'. His needs were for 'reassurance, regular supervision and feedback plus slow, small-stepped curriculum' within a situation 'where he will receive the maximum amount of stimulation, and where he can acquire basic skills of literacy, numeracy and language by carefully graded steps and short-term feedback. Requires ESN-M school as soon as possible'.

It was reported by the medical officer and head teacher that Jonathan's parents were very co-operative and anxious to help. This was also acknowledged in the educational psychologist's report, where references were made to their ability and readiness to promote Jonathan's growth and development, and to their level of support and interest in their son. However, the psychologist also felt that the child had been over-protected, commenting: 'Mother very over-protective, appears to be highly anxious and lacking in confidence herself'. There had, according to this report, been some opposition from the parents to the transfer, although no reference was made to this by the head teacher, nor in the parental interview reported later in this chapter.

Following transfer the reports from the special school show a remarkable consistency. In each of his primary years he was described as lacking application, being timid and reserved in his dealings with peers, and as being apathetic and easily led. However, by the time he was 12 Jonathan appeared to be taking more interest in his work and making more progress. His report indicated a slight improvement in reading, writing and number work.

In reading he needed constant repetition of letter sounds and blends but his ability to build up words was improving slowly. On the whole the teacher reported a 'pleasing year's work'. His written work had also improved, although 'he needed to be pushed all the way in order to complete work given to him'. In number work he had completed three of the four rules of number and was working on the fourth, division. He had put much effort into his number work during that year. Overall, he was described as a very pleasant and polite member of the class, and the head teacher's report concluded that he had worked well all year.

His school report at the end of the following year indicated that his progress had continued. 'More than a slight improvement' had taken place in his reading, where he was said to have made a consistent effort. He read carefully and understood most of what he read. His written work had only improved slightly and it was reported that he still worked very slowly. Nevertheless, his comprehension work was rated as quite good and showing much thought. His work in numbers was steady and had showed a slight improvement. He had a sound understanding of money and time. Overall he was described as 'always well behaved and helpful' and 'had a good sense of humour', and the head teacher had concluded that he had been most consistent in his efforts to improve.

Jonathan transferred, as a consequence of the closure of his special school, to the fourth year of a local comprehensive school. This was the school chosen by his parents, and agreed by the educational psychologist. His special school was not involved in the decision, and was uncertain about his coping in the ordinary school, arguing that in general terms he was a very dozy, lethargic character who liked to do inactive things: 'He needs a steamroller' to push him along.

TIMOTHY

Timothy was first referred to the schools psychological service at the age of 4.6. At that time he had a reported IQ of 67 and a developmental age of 3.9. The educational psychologist's view was that he was 'an immature child who is both socially and linguistically deprived' and recommended him for placement in an ESN-M school.

Timothy experienced considerable disruption in his early years, and following the recommendation he was repeatedly taken into care and fostered by several families. As a consequence the recommendation was not implemented. Instead he spent periods in several infant schools. He was referred again at the age of 8 for slow progress. He was again recommended for transfer to an ESN-M school on the basis of poor reading comprehension and fluency. His practical, creative and physical skills and co-ordination were reported as only fair, and he was felt to lack basic love and affection.

Despite his turbulent early years Timothy's relationships with adults and children were considered good, and he displayed no special characteristics such as solitary behaviour, timidity or moodiness. His behavioural and emotional development were reported to be normal. It was established that although he was visually impaired he had not worn spectacles during his early years.

His mother was in favour of Timothy's transfer to ESN-M school, and at 8½ years old he transferred. In his primary years at the school his reports were very consistent. He lacked application, was timid in his relations with peers and yet was categorized as a leader. From his reports for the final two years before transfer from his ESN-M school it is clear that Timothy had most problems in language. His first report claimed that although he was a good reader he needed to read more slowly in order to gain understanding. His written work had improved only slightly; his teacher claimed that he could work much harder than he had been doing. His comprehension work was described as fair. His work in maths was evidently of better quality. His results were rated good and he was putting 'much more effort here than in English work'. In general he was thought to be well behaved but could be silly at times.

By the end of his final year his reading had improved to the extent that he had mastered most of the necessary skills in reading and was well on the way to becoming a fluent reader. Improvement in written work was slight, although his creative writing showed a vivid imagination. His number work was again good—he had completed and revised all four rules—and he had no problems telling the time. His general behaviour appeared to have matured. He was seen as a pleasant, polite and helpful member of the group.

Timothy was in the same special school as Jonathan and had to transfer because the school was closing. His parents chose a local comprehensive, not the same as that chosen by Jonathan's parents. This led to an assessment by the educational psychologist. At the age of 14.4 he had a reading age of 8.5. Nevertheless, the report concluded:

> Small for his age but socially confident. Having developed a narrow range of skills which meet his requirements in a relationship. He thus appears 'old headed' but very adequate and is apparently fairly popular with his peers. Intellectually (WISC-R) Timothy is borderline ESN-M but his reading and number are adequate for the remedial department of his local high school. He is reported to be a well behaved boy at his special school and to me seemed very conformist. I consider that Timothy's mother's request for transfer to the high school is a reasonable request and I recommend that he attends the high school after summer for his remaining two years.

SARAH

Sarah's learning difficulties were evident at infant school. Lack of improvement prompted her parents to send her to a private school where it was hoped she would benefit from working in smaller groups. The conditions at the school appeared conducive to learning. Sarah worked within her own age group of ten children and, in addition, received individual attention. Despite this the head teacher commented that 'she has made very little progress and only appears to recognize words by size and shape. She fails to join sounds'. Her comprehension was weak and she was unable, in spelling, to retain recognition. In a recent test of four-letter words Sarah had scored none out of 30. It was also noted that she had little numerical understanding.

The head teacher concluded her report by stating that, 'after a reasonable period of time, and with a considerable amount of individual attention, it became increasingly apparent that Sarah could only progress if she received special education'. Following an interview at the school her stepfather referred her to the psychological service.

The medical officer noted no physical factors relevant to her learning difficulties, and the educational psychologist described her as 'not unintelligent' on the basis of her assessment. On the WISC-R her verbal quotient was 87, her performance quotient 100 and her full scale IQ of 92. Note was particularly taken of her low scores on the sub-tests of information and reading, although overall her verbal and performance scores 'fell within the normal range'. The educational psychologist also considered that Sarah had visual memory and psychomotor problems. The report was extensive and concluded, as had the head teacher, that Sarah was probably dyslexic. 'Sarah has specific learning difficulties and is probably mildly dyslexic. She also has psychomotor problems and in particular is not learning how to form her letters correctly. She still confuses b's and d's and will sometimes become completely confused, e.g. when asked to write the word "from" she wrote "gone". Sarah also has a very poor visual memory and a very poor retention of learning, especially rote learning. Occasionally Sarah mispronounces words by shortening them, e.g. she will say "terial" for "material" and "member" for "remember". She also has verbal sequencing problems'. Further testing established that she was one year behind in reading and spelling.

Although it was noted that Sarah's mother, on her own admission, had been very over-protective and over-indulgent of her child, particularly after the break-up of her first marriage, parental attitudes were described as being good. They were interested and supportive, understood their daughter's difficulties and were keen to do what they could to help her. Despite this, Sarah was painfully aware of her slow progress and learning difficulties and became reluctant to attend school, partly as a consequence of the fact that her peers were beginning to ridicule her. In consideration of all these factors it was recommended that she transfer to an ESN-M school shortly before her eighth birthday.

The reports on Sarah from the special school were extensive and thorough. The extracts selected here give a flavour of Sarah's progress in the three years before her re-integration into ordinary school at the age of 11.

The report at the end of her first year was very satisfactory. Steady progress had been made in reading, even though she still had visual problems and some letter reversal. She had more difficulties with writing. She could cope with simple sentences but her spelling and grammar retention were poor. Orally, however, she was good. Her number work improved but she was prone to make careless mistakes. She knew basic shapes and time in hours and half-hours, but she was 'still at the concrete operational level of comprehension'. In the classroom she was said to be a good, polite child who worked well, and her attitude to the teacher was 'very well mannered and keen to please'. Out of class, however, she could be bossy and 'stir up trouble with other girls'. The concluding comment of her report was: 'Steady progress made. A potential transfer.'

The following year's report indicated further progress in reading although she could be erratic and needed work on spellings and phonics. She had started free writing and could compose two or three sentences. Her written work was neat and her letter formation good. She continued making careless mistakes in number work but was apparently progressing satisfactorily. Her behaviour in class continued to be good, although she tended to chatter at times. She was reported as being 'polite, helpful and mature in manner', and her out of class behaviour was good 'most of the time'. The concluding comment implied that she could do better. 'Sarah has a lot going for her but she seems content to be in the top group in the class, and not to extend herself.'

During the following, penultimate, year of her stay at the ESN-M school Sarah's parents began to probe the possibility of re-integration. In a letter to the school her mother argued that Sarah was aware of the social stigma attached to the school, and stated that they were anxious that she did not stay there any longer than was necessary. Despite this they indicated that they were aware of possible difficulties if Sarah transferred too early. In reply the school argued that it was too early to consider transfer and that she needed to consolidate the progress being made. Nevertheless, it was their intention to request re-assessment the following year.

By the end of the year, although her work was showing evidence of reading for meaning, it was felt that 'Sarah could make greater progress if she attended school more regularly, extended herself in school, and was prepared to read at home and learn new words on her reading card'. Her written work showed evidence of continuing progress, however, and she was able to compose some very good pieces of work. She was working well in number work and was capable of abstract thought. She had grasped the concept of multiplication and was now working on division. Her behaviour continued to be good, and her attitude mature, presenting as a 'happy, friendly girl who wants to help'. Nevertheless, a lack of effort continued to be perceived.

Her final report indicated steady progress in reading although it was suggested that she should extend her reading experience at home to widen her vocabulary. Sarah was reported as enjoying her writing. Her punctuation and spelling were improving. She was very competent orally and was described as an 'excellent actress'. In number work she could compute in the four rules but lacked application skills. Structure appeared to be important here: 'Each new shape has to be carefully structured as she is easily confused.' Her behaviour in class continued to be good, and she was described as 'positive, reliable, friendly, co-operative'. Lack of effort was again a concluding point. 'Mother is anxious for Sarah to attend a comprehensive school. She should be able to cope in the remedial department at [girls' comprehensive school], but she will have to work with greater enthusiasm and make a greater effort with homework.'

Sarah transferred, at the age of 11, into the first year of a local comprehensive school.

PETER

Peter's difficulties in school were a by-product of his parents' lifestyle. They had led a roaming, nomadic life, and by the age of 8 he had attended 15 schools. He was referred to the educational psychologist at the age of 8.2 after being in his current junior school for only one month. At that time he was in a second year mixed ability class with no remedial provision. However, the head teacher had been teaching him sounds and keywords from the Ladybird scheme. He had read book 1a, but was having difficulty with 2a because he confused words beginning with the same letter, e.g. he could not distinguish between 'the' and 'this', or 'fun' and 'fish'. The school had assessed his reading age on a Schonell test as being three years below his chronological age. The head teacher considered that he was 'severely backward, cannot read, knows no sounds ... reverses letters when writing. Free writing unreadable'. The class teacher was equally concerned, feeling that without specialist help Peter's failure could become permanent, and that it was impossible for her to give him the attention he needed. Interestingly, it was noted that his basic number work and bonds were quite good, and that he could use money adequately.

When tested by the educational psychologist, Peter's WISC-R verbal scale score was 91, performance 87 and full scale IQ 88. The BAS reading test confirmed his reading age as 5.4, and he was assessed as having a spelling age of 6.1. Most of the WISC sub-test scores were within the normal range, and he achieved a higher than average score in the mental arithmetic sub-test. His lowest score was in the information sub-test, which reflects a very poor general knowledge. The report concluded that 'Peter is within the normal range of ability but has probably missed much education due to the movements of his family'.

With regard to behaviour, the head teacher regarded Peter as friendly and pleasant but having a shy manner with adults. Similarly, the educational psychologist described him as a rather quiet, co-operative boy who was a little more fidgety than most children in the assessment situation. He noted that Peter did not seem to dislike school but that he was 'far behind the average for his group and has missed so much school I don't consider his chances of catching up very great if he remains in normal school'. He thus recommended that 'a temporary period in a day ESN-M school would be more appropriate to his present needs'.

Difficulty in contacting Peter's mother delayed the transfer until the following September, when he was 9, although this did not mean that the situation remained the same. A teacher from the reading and language service assisted Peter in his ordinary school until the transfer.

Some improvement evidently took place during his year in junior school because on entry to ESN-M school he had a reading age of 6 and was reported to be reading well and competently on *Kathy and Mark* book 4. His written work was quite good although note was made of letter reversals. His number work was good: 'He can tackle addition, subtraction, and multiplication without concrete aids.' His behaviour was rated as quite good although he resented being reprimanded. His class teacher concluded: 'Peter responds well to encouragement and success and should hopefully make satisfactory progress. A tendency, however, to mix with children who may lead him along a deviant path.'

By the end of the first year his reading age had advanced to 7.9, and good progress was recorded. His written work was also good, and he could compose several sentences with ease although his writing was very small. In number he could work with hundreds, tens and units in all four rules, compute addition and multiplication with carrying, and his work on measurement and money was good. His behaviour was good, but he was talkative and restless, and occasionally 'moody if told off'. Nevertheless, he was seen as a 'friendly, cheerful boy', who had the ability to do well, particularly if he could overcome his moods.

At the end of his final junior year his teacher reported excellent progress in reading, where he now had a reading age of 8.6 and a spelling age of 7.7. He produced interesting writing in a logical sequence, had good communication skills and excellent acting ability. In number work he was able to work accurately and grasp new concepts quickly. He was keen and enthusiastic and was able to work on the four rules on hundreds, tens and units with carrying, and long division with remainders. He could tell the time to the minute and his money work was good. He was above average in games and had a special interest in boxing. In class his behaviour was excellent and he was reported as co-operative, helpful and reliable. His attitude to work was also excellent and he was anxious to improve. The only negative comment related to his occasionally ganging up on others in the playground. The conclusion read: 'Peter has had to cope with emotional problems at home during the last few months but mother finds him very supportive. She is anxious for him to attend a comprehensive school in September. He should be able to cope in mainstream education and a place at [a local comprehensive school] is to be requested when the educational psychologist has made his recommendations.'

Peter transferred into the first year of a comprehensive school at the age of 11.

ANNA

Anna was the third of four daughters in a family described as being supportive, stable and insightful, and a little perplexed by Anna's unpredictable attitudes and intolerance of the frustrations that arise from learning problems. She was first referred at the age of 6½, but records of that referral are thin. She continued in her ordinary school, but was referred again at the age of 9.

At that time the head teacher reported that her attendance was regular and that she had received individual attention throughout her school career. Her reading was described as quite good although her score on the Burt test indicated that her reading age was one year less than her chronological age. Her spelling was less good. She had a poor grasp of mathematical concepts, which was attributed to a poor memory. She knew, as a result of learning by rote, her tables up to four and could compute in addition and subtraction using tens and units with carrying. In more practical areas she had poor fine skills and made innovative illustrations. Her physical skills and co-ordination were poor.

Anna's major problem, however, was her behaviour, which was described as domineering and egocentric. Her class teacher said that Anna demanded immediate attention and that her social relationships were poor. 'Anna sits alone as she upsets other children ... she must be first and pushes them out of the way.' The teacher felt that the acceptance of her behaviour by her classmates was on the wane. 'Anna has been with this set of children for five years and has been accepted and helped, but I have seen signs of rejection by her peers ... especially in group activities and games. She has no peer friendships and drifts from group to group at playtimes and is teased and exploited by older children at times.'

Anna was first assessed by a physiotherapist, who concluded: 'Her initial assessment revealed she had poor gross co-ordination affecting balance and general mobility. Poor eye/hand control affecting ball throwing and catching, poor fine co-ordination affecting her manipulative skills. She also had a short attention span and difficulty recognizing shapes.'

The psychological assessment two weeks later indicated a WISC-R verbal score of 84 but a much lower performance score of 69. The psychologist noted that: 'Her "automatic" use and range of vocabulary was quite like that of a child of her age but its application to reasoning and comprehension was weak. That is, Anna can project a chatty veneer of ability but has difficulty in applying it to solving problems and generating a new understanding. Anna's non-verbal, mechanical problem-solving skill is, at the present, restricted in a similar way to her verbal reasoning and comprehension. Anna has a good eye for appropriate and essential detail, she can label it but is not so good at manipulating the information to solve problems.' It was thought that the development of verbal reasoning and comprehension, and non-verbal problem solving, would be important elements in a special school programme. A further assessment by the medical officer reported handicaps in vision, behaviour, emotional and intellectual development. Anna's squint was being treated and the prognosis was that it would improve, but the move to a local special school was supported on the basis of her abnormal behaviour.

The general opinion seemed to be that Anna could probably cope at her primary school but that, without some special placement, she would be unlikely to do so in secondary school. As the head teacher reported: 'Whilst Anna is fully accepted here she nevertheless stands out as being odd. In a large secondary school this will inevitably unearth problems', particularly in the light of her reactions to criticism or teasing, which could be extreme.

Anna transferred to a local special school at the age of 9.3. Records of Anna's progress in the special school indicated that her reading was very good, her comprehension skills good and that she was able to work unaided. The only negative comment related to her poor punctuation in writing. Anna's performance in number work was poor and her 'weakest link'.

It was her behaviour which was of most concern. This was reported as obsessive in that she 'sets a pattern and follows it through' and 'gets angry' and 'frustrated' at times. The teacher pointed out that when Anna first arrived at special school she had 'insisted on being first at everything', but has 'been much improved'. Nevertheless, she still 'does not relate to others', is 'selfish, totally unaware of others' and 'doesn't see her faults'. She 'likes to think she's best' and is 'isolated' from her peers.

Anna's teacher did not think that Anna had been correctly placed in ESN-M school because her difficulties were social rather than academic. Ironically, the teacher considered that Anna's isolation and egocentricity might actually get her through ordinary school. Thus, although she expected her to meet with problems after transfer, she thought she would cope.

Anna transferred at the age of 11 into the first year of a comprehensive school.

PARENTAL PERSPECTIVES

Early behaviour

There were few commonalities between the early experiences of these five children. Having Timothy at 17, and a husband who drank, Timothy's mother had found it difficult to cope and had not always been able to care properly for him. Of all the five children, Timothy experienced most disruption in his early years. He was repeatedly taken into care and fostered by a number of different families. His early education was spent in several infant schools, culminating in a final spell at his local infant school when he had been returned to his mother. At this time, in his mother's words, he 'hated school' and was a reluctant attender. 'We used to drag him.'

While his mother felt she had no control over him, his teacher found him withdrawn. His mother explained: 'He'd sit in a corner as if like you'd leathered him.' Compounding the problem was the mother's poor relationship with staff at the school and her belief that the school was at least partly to blame for his hatred of it. For example, when Timothy began wetting himself at school, he told his mother it was because the teacher would not let him go to the toilet. In view of his withdrawn behaviour at infant school, it is not surprising that Timothy failed to progress.

Although Peter's early education was also disrupted, he was not simultaneously subjected to disruption in his home life. Peter's father was a gypsy and although his mother was not, they travelled together as a family. His attendance at school was therefore erratic. 'He's not really been in infant school at all properly.... He just went odd days, odd weeks', said his mother. When Peter's mother and father separated, he settled with his mother and brother in a town and began attending junior school regularly. However, having missed much of the basics he was a long way behind his peers. Although given special, individual, tuition from his head teacher, he was ultimately referred to the schools psychological service.

Although disrupted early schooling might possibly be seen as a cause of some of Timothy's, and all of Peter's, difficulties this was not the case with other children in the sample. Jonathan, Sarah and Anna all had a normal infant school experience. Neither Jonathan's nor Sarah's parents had anticipated that their children would experience difficulties at school. When Jonathan was 3½ the health visitor had suggested to his mother that he should be talking more, but since he was the first child in the family his mother had not noticed anything untoward. He had attended play school and 'enjoyed every minute of it'. Although he tended to be a quiet child his nursery school teachers had said he played well. Given this it is surprising that his introduction to early schooling did not run equally smoothly. It did, in fact, prove to be a rather traumatic experience for him, and initially he had wet the bed. His birthday was at the end of August and he started school at the age of 4½, which his mother thought had perhaps been too soon for him. Another year would have given him a little more time to mature.

Nevertheless, after a shaky start Jonathan had settled down and his parents thought his first and second years at infant school had been satisfactory. It was not until he began junior school that his parents became aware that he was finding school difficult. It was the emotional difficulties Jonathan was facing rather than problems with school work that first became apparent. 'He seemed', said his father, 'to take a lot of stick in the playground.' Jonathan had become the butt of jokes and teasing, particularly from those whose acquaintance he first made at infant school. Not surprisingly Jonathan became withdrawn and reluctant to attend school. 'I used to leave him at school crying his eyes out', said his mother.

When it became evident that Jonathan also had learning difficulties in his second year at infant school his parents had searched for a cause of his slow progress. They thought he might be colour blind and had his eyesight checked. Although he was not colour blind he was found to be very short-sighted. His parents' search for a cause of his difficulties was not limited to physical possibilities. His mother also examined retrospectively and critically her own parenting, thinking that she may have been in some way responsible for Jonathan's problems. She thought, for example, that she might not have spent enough time with him as a baby.

All the parents described, directly or indirectly, a gulf in feeling, knowledge and understanding between themselves and professionals, and it seems that while the latter may have attempted to tend to the child's needs, the needs of the parents were neglected. The obvious area for parents to examine when looking for possible causes was their own parenting. Yet the self-criticism and blame some parents apportioned to themselves often seemed unwarranted.

Sarah's learning difficulties became apparent at infant school. Within three months of her starting school her mother was informed of this. There was, nevertheless, no improvement, so when Sarah was 8 her mother decided to send her to a private school where she hoped that she would benefit from smaller classes and specialized tuition. In the event the latter turned out not to be available and her learning difficulties did not decrease. Her form teacher suggested that Sarah might be dyslexic, but her mother was less sure, and instead suspected that her problems may have been associated with the insecurity of being brought up in a broken home. Sarah's mother and father had separated shortly after their daughter's birth. Like Jonathan and Timothy, however, Sarah's learning difficulties were coupled with a general unhappiness at school. She did not like or want to go to school and it was suggested to her mother that she might be happier elsewhere. Her mother thus felt that she had no choice but to go along with the school's suggestion that Sarah be referred to the schools psychological service.

From a very early age it was clear to Anna's parents, who had two older daughters, that Anna's behaviour was abnormal. They described her at the ages of 2 and 3 years as being like a wild animal. Not only was she hyperactive, she was also obsessive, extremely wilful, aggressive and at times violent. Her mother had, for example, great difficulty putting nappies on her, although these were necessary because Anna wet the bed. Her mother described the typical scene: 'It would be a physical battle, she would bite and nip and kick. You had to impose your will on her, but it was very, very difficult. And something like that would just blow up out of nothing. One minute she'd be perfectly okay and all of a sudden there's this kicking and screaming and biting.' At times it was necessary for them to harness her to her bed. Her obsessive behaviour was equally taxing, as her father explained: 'Her mind in those days ... seemed to have little pegs that she hung her day on and if she didn't know that her mother was going out shopping or something of that sort, then as soon as the breakfast pots were washed up and put away, the next little peg she hung the day on was lunch, which meant of course that the table had to be laid immediately for lunch, so as fast as her mother was putting away the breakfast pots, Anna would be getting things out and literally throwing things on the table. Her mother would say: "no, it's not time yet to lay the table for lunch, we'll pop those away for now", but as fast as she was putting them away, Anna would be getting them out, so in the end she would just take an armful of crockery and out it would go. She would end up throwing things because that's the next thing her mind moved to.'

Anna had been born with a number of physical problems, a twisted foot, a squint and a small hole in the top of her head which was skinned over but marked by a very slight indentation. It looked very much like a forceps mark although labour had not been induced and forceps had not been used. The hole had worried both parents but no one explained to them what it was or what had caused it, despite constant questions. As Anna became older the hole became a source of irritation to her. 'It used to irritate her and she would scratch it and it would bleed leaving scabs on her head.'

The silence Anna's parents met when they asked questions about this hole was like that they faced when they asked questions about the possible causes of Anna's behaviour and difficulties. Anna's mother said: 'Nobody, nobody will say anything.... We've been everywhere, but nobody will.' These experiences led them to believe that the professionals they encountered were unwilling to be frank about their diagnoses. Indeed, in all parental interviews there was a clearly perceived line between themselves and the professionals. The latter had the power to transmit information, or in some cases to control situations and determine outcomes, while the parents were cast into the role of receivers. The fact that professionals had the power to exclude parents from information they believed they had a right to know, and to determine the future of their child, was bitterly resented. Parents were uneasy that control of their child's fate was in the hands of those who knew their child less well than they did themselves, for whom their child was only one of a large number, and who might not have only their child's interests at heart. This feeling had come from their experience with the system. Those who had started out with a trust in the wisdom of professionals had learned otherwise. It seemed as though they had realized that they had a deeper knowledge of their child than the professionals, and seemed critical of the lack of more penetrating insights than they themselves already held. The net result was that some, like the parents of Anna and Sarah, demonstrated a greater confidence in their own assessments of their child than in those given. In short, there was a common sense of disillusionment with the system, and on a very personal level, with the professionals who operated it. The people they hoped would be able to help them and their child had tended to disappoint them. Scepticism was rife. Professionals of all types were rarely described as being helpful or even useful. At times, as in the following example, they were portrayed as doing more damage than good. Anna's father described his wife and daughter's meeting with a child psychiatrist.

> Anna's mother was feeling low and feeling that nobody was really giving any help or support and I said to the GP: 'Is there nowhere else? Because we'll take her anywhere in the country if you can give us some help for this child.' And the only name she could give us was a child psychiatrist. Went there ... he was a very caring person ... but in the first interview he confronted Anna with all her problems. We'd played them down all those years. Maths had always been the biggest problem.... He asked Anna if she liked maths, 'Yes', she said: 'Are you good at maths?', he said 'Yes', she said: 'No you're not', he said, 'you're rubbish'. Anna's mother was really upset, he really confronted her with everything, you know: 'These are your problems, you've got to face up to them.' He set about, in our opinion, destroying that child, certainly destroying all the attitudes that we'd tried to inculcate. Anna's mother was distressed beyond all measure.

It was not only the child psychiatrist's approach that Anna's parents were unhappy with. Later in the interview Anna's mother described other examples: 'I used to go to a behavioural specialist. She was absolutely useless, all she did was upset the child even further. She hadn't a clue. When she signed her off I saw two other doctors. One said, "by the time she is 10 she will be normal", and the other one said, "oh, a long time before that". Now fortunately I never believed that because I knew my child better than they did.'

On such recommendations Anna attended play school, but seemed unable to play.

Instead she simply disrupted the play of other children, as her father explained: 'The only thing she could do was to be disruptive, spoil whatever they were doing.'

PLACEMENT IN SPECIAL SCHOOL

Timothy's transfer from special to ordinary school had not been discussed with his parents. It had been dealt with by social workers. Fortunately his mother had no reservations about the transfer. She herself had attended the same special school and was confident and happy that this would be an appropriate placement for her son. The head of the special school had invited her to visit the school before Timothy began.

A similar situation seems to have arisen in Peter's case. His mother recalled that she had not been invited to the ordinary school to discuss Peter's difficulties, or the possibility of transfer. Discussions had simply taken place between the special and the ordinary school and she had been asked whether she had any objections. She had initially been uncertain whether it was in Peter's interests to agree to the move or not. It was only after looking round the school that she decided in favour of the transfer.

In the remaining three cases the possibility of transfer to special school was carefully discussed with the child's parents before contact was made with the special school. Nevertheless, although this may have made them feel more involved in the process, it had clearly not always made them feel that they had a degree of control over events, or that they were able to make a choice. The options open to them were restricted and often consisted of only one, transfer to special school. Sarah's case was typical. Sarah was finding life at private school difficult both academically and socially, and the school itself seemed to be finding it difficult to deal adequately with her needs. At the school's suggestion she was referred to the psychological service and found to have a reading age two or three years behind her chronological age of 8. The school suggested to her mother that Sarah might be happier at another school. An educational psychologist saw Sarah on three or four occasions and concluded that she did need special education. Although her learning difficulties were specific and she was described in the report as being 'probably mildly dyslexic', it was suggested that she be transferred to what was then an ESN-M school. Her mother was reluctant to agree to the transfer because of the stigma attached to the school, but when it was made clear that there was no other suitable school within daily travelling distance she realized that she had no alternative. She was not willing to consider sending Sarah to a boarding school.

Sarah's mother felt that the difficulty she had in coming to terms with having to send Sarah to ESN-M school was confounded by the attitude of the head teacher of that school. Having had the experience of having her daughter rejected by two ordinary schools and feeling that her daughter really did not deserve the stigma of having to attend ESN-M school, she found to her horror and confusion that the ESN-M school might also see fit to reject her. 'So there's me deciding whether I'm going to send her there and on Wednesday the head said, "Well it all depends on whether we can accept Sarah". It was like trying to get her into some exclusive school. I was absolutely amazed. There was me thinking I was doing them a favour sending her, and he left me in no doubt that he'd have to think whether she was suitable.' She was accepted by the school and sent reluctantly by her mother who believed that Sarah would 'be out within the year'. This impression was reinforced by Sarah's new form teacher who told her that she could not understand why Sarah had been sent to the school and that she would be out of the school 'in fifteen months'. However, this did not turn out to be the case.

The possibility of transfer to special school was also discussed with Jonathan's parents before any action was taken. The school had made a considerable effort to keep Jonathan but he was finding life increasingly difficult. When transfer to ESN-M school was recommended by the head teacher his parents agreed on the basis that if it was going to help him then it had to be the right decision.

Although Anna's case was akin to that of Sarah and Jonathan it was unique in that the suggestion of transfer was first raised by her parents rather than by the school. They had played a proactive rather than passive or reactive role in Anna's education throughout. Anna's mother had taught in a primary school for four years before the birth of her first child. Possibly the knowledge of the system gained from this experience gave them the confidence to take this kind of role. They were under no illusions about what the system could do for Anna and what it might be able to offer her. Hence they adopted a proactive stance. From the beginning they regarded the comments made and advice given by professionals with open minds, rather than treating them as being absolute. Put simply, they were aware at the outset, as other parents seemed unaware, that professionals could be wrong. Their attitude was summed up by Anna's father: 'Over the years what we have done is talk to anyone who will talk to us, anyone with any sort of expertise that just could have some bearing. But we've never ever accepted what they've said, we've always discussed it ourselves and then said, "well, okay, fine, they may have got a point there [or] well, what a load of rubbish or whatever", and we've been able between us to pick out the things which we felt were useful, constructive and we've built on those.'

Thus Anna's parents had kept very close contact with the ordinary primary school from the moment Anna began attending it. 'We didn't leave it to them. We were determined that no one was going to leave Anna sitting in a corner at the back and ignore her. They were going to try and get as much out of her as they could.' They worked closely with the school, which in turn provided materials for them to use with Anna at home. Nevertheless, although they were able to bring Anna within two years of her peers academically, they found it difficult to close the gap further. Their decision to raise the issue of Anna's scholastic future at the age of 9 was based on two factors. First, disregarding her social difficulties, academically Anna was well behind her peers. Anna's two elder sisters, already attending the local comprehensive school, were being given work that they knew Anna would be unable to cope with, and as mixed ability classes operated in the first three years, they saw no reason to suppose that the type of work being given to the two older girls would be any different from that which would be given to Anna. Discipline, which they felt was lax at the secondary school, also caused them concern. Although this did not present major problems for Anna's sisters, they felt it could create problems for a child like Anna. Secondly, in her final year at her primary school she was to be taught by a teacher in whom they had little confidence. Thus it seemed appropriate to consider Anna's future then rather than later. 'We decided that there was no way she would go to a normal secondary school, so if we were going to transfer her somewhere else we may as well do it at 9 to avoid this class teacher, than to do it at 11.'

As in Sarah's case it was felt that there was not a school in the locality that could meet Anna's needs. The opinion of the professionals involved was that the ESN-M school was the only one likely to come close to the ideal, although they had reservations because they felt her attainments and IQ were slightly above those of children normally admitted to the school. The possibility of residential placement was considered but discounted. It was felt that this would be too temporary a measure, both from Anna's point of view and from that of her family, for the effects to be positive.

Anna's parents felt that they considered every possibility, in terms of appropriate placement, and not the professionals, who suggested no type of placement other than ESN-M school. One possibility considered was keeping Anna at her primary school and then transferring her at 11 to one particular secondary school, which had a remedial department. Here they felt that Anna might be able to cope and, moreover, that the school might be able to cope with Anna. However, the educational psychologist was dismissive, saying: 'If she ends up in the remedial department at the secondary school she'll be mixing with the same riff-raff that she'll be mixing with at the special school.'

The awareness that a wholly satisfactory conclusion to the case was unlikely because there was not a school suited to Anna's needs within daily travelling distance led the LEA to leave the ultimate decision-making to Anna's parents. With residential placement discounted the number of alternatives amounted only to two—either to leave Anna at her ordinary primary school or to transfer her to special school. After visiting the special school and feeling that Anna would probably fit in quite well there Anna's parents made the decision that their daughter should transfer.

Chapter 4

The Integration Process.
II: Curriculum Experiences

INTRODUCTION

Having considered how and why these five children found themselves in special schools we now turn to the core issue—their re-integration into the ordinary sector. In considering this process, and its effects, we felt that information was needed which was relevant to the following five central questions.

1. What were the children's experiences of curriculum on either side of the transfer? To what extent was there any continuity?
2. What were the children's reactions to their work on either side of the transfer? Were they, for example, equally involved in their work in both settings?
3. Was there any indication that work was more appropriate in one setting than the other?
4. What were the immediate and longer term effects of re-integration in terms of academic performance and social integration?
5. What of the process of integration itself? Was it well organized, did appropriate liaison take place, was the organizational provision in the ordinary school appropriate, did the teachers themselves believe they had the skills necessary to teach such children?

These questions structure the shape of the following chapters as they are addressed for each child. Although each child is dealt with individually the five are grouped into two pairs and a single. Jonathan and Timothy were in the same special school class but transferred to different comprehensive schools. This was also the case for Sarah and Peter in a different LEA, leaving Anna as the single case.

The data necessary to address these questions were collected by various means from various sources. In order to allow consideration of the children's curriculum experiences the teachers in both the special and ordinary schools agreed to provide examples that, in their view, sampled the range and quality of work undertaken. In addition the teachers were interviewed about curriculum matters, including schemes of work adopted, general teaching approach and so on. Analyses of these data allowed a description of the curriculum sampled, and a comparison of curriculum across transfer.

Children's reactions to their work were assessed by observation and interview. They were observed in mathematics and language lessons at three stages in the integration process: in the final term of their special school, and in the first and third terms of their ordinary schools. At each stage it was planned to observe two lessons in each subject, but this was not always achieved because of pupil absence, lesson cancellation and the like.

For the purpose of these observations a pupil-focused observation schedule was designed specifically for this study. Following extensive pilot work a category system was devised, centring on the extent, nature and type of pupil involvement (see Appendix I). From these categories eight general categories were derived which are described below. The schedule was designed to be coded continuously to avoid data loss, and also allowed multiple coding, to reflect classroom action more accurately. For example, it was possible to code the pupil who might be attending to the teacher's task instructions but at the same time had his or her hand raised to attract the teacher's attention.

As stated above, eight general categories were derived, five concerning on-task behaviour and three off-task. These are defined as follows:

On task
1. Individual work. Instances where the child is fully involved in the task but working individually.
2. Attending to teacher. Here the child is fully involved in listening to teacher talk. This talk could involve an instruction, an explanation or a demonstration. Copying from the blackboard would also be considered here.
3. Peer interaction. Interactions between peers, either initiated or responded to, that relate to the task being worked.
4. Requesting teacher help or feedback. Where the child requests, or attempts to request, help from the teacher relating to instructions, explanations, materials or feedback on work done.
5. Organizing materials. Instances where the child acquires, or organizes, the materials appropriate to the task set.

Off task
1. Not attending. Not attending occurs for several reasons, including passive staring into space or watching others, physical confrontations or leaving the classroom without permission.
2. Attending to non-task teacher talk. Attends to talk that does not relate to the task set.
3. Peer interaction. Initiates or responds to peer talk not related to the task.

In addition to the systematic observations an attempt was made, within the time available, to acquire data on which to base judgements of task appropriateness. The method for obtaining these data followed closely that presented in Bennett *et al.* (1987). For each task observed the following information was gained:

How the teacher presented and specified the task.
How the class was organized.

A description of the task set.
How the pupil carried out the work.
Any difficulties encountered, their nature and type.
A description of the completed task.

These observations were again limited to mathematics and language tasks.

Extensive interviews with the children, their teachers and their parents provided information relevant to the children's academic and social integration, and to the process of integration itself.

JONATHAN AND TIMOTHY

Special school

Curriculum

It will be recalled that Jonathan and Timothy were in the same special school class. The maths and language curriculum in this class is first portrayed before we consider their work involvement and indications of task appropriateness. Their transfer to different secondary schools is then considered before we present the curriculum and their involvement in it in their first and third terms.

Mathematics   Table 4.1 characterizes the curriculum from an analysis of the samples of tasks provided by the special school.

Table 4.1. *Maths curriculum in the special school.*

Addition	Computation	HTU
	Problems	HTU
Subtraction	Computation	HTU
	Problems	HTU
Multiplication	Computation	HTU
	Problems	HTU
Division	Computation	HTU
	Problems	—
Money		Counting, change to £5
Time		Telling, to 1 minute, problems

No particular mathematics scheme was used and the curriculum cover was largely restricted to the four rules, money and time. Both boys had done work on three of the four rules earlier in the year and by the end of the year were computing division sums with remainders. Both had done work on money, particularly on counting and giving change, and both were reported as proficient in this. Both could tell the time and were attempting problems of the type: 'What time is 35 minutes later than ten to one?'

Table 4.2. *Language work.*

Comprehension	Sentence completion: missing words, SRA cards
Grammar	Through *Sound Sense* (Tansley)
Recording	Mainly through a diary
Story writing	Various topics
Phonics	Blends such as 'pl', 'oo', 'sl', 'ch'
Reading	Ginn 360, Ladybird as supplementary
Handwriting	Formation of individual letters

Language   The work in language covered by Jonathan and Timothy is shown in Table 4.2. Both displayed difficulties in this area. Timothy's grammar was very weak, and his writing took the form of a continuous stream of words. Full stops, where used, were inappropriately placed, and other forms of punctuation were not used at all. His use of tenses was also erratic. His spelling was very poor, even though the teacher demanded the rewriting of each spelling error. However, his handwriting was reasonable and well spaced. Despite Timothy's difficulties with writing his teacher noted that his writing could be very creative, utilizing what she regarded as a 'vivid imagination'. His teacher had noted a slight improvement in his reading and felt that he was 'well on the way to becoming a fluent reader'. Nevertheless, his reading age trailed his chronological age by three years.

Jonathan too was reported to have made progress but still remained weak in sentence construction and handwriting. His ideas were often well ordered but he rarely used capitals or paragraphs. His spelling was fair, his vocabulary limited and his work always very slow. His reading appeared somewhat better and he showed reasonable understanding.

Task involvement

The profiles of task involvement of Jonathan and Timothy are shown in Table 4.3.

Table 4.3. *Task involvement: Jonathan and Timothy. Figures are the percentage of time spent on each activity.*

	Timothy		Jonathan	
	Language	Maths	Language	Maths
On task				
Individual work	40.4	70.9	66.9	60.4
Attending to teacher	15.3	7.7	2.9	7.8
Peer interaction	4.5	2.7	0.3	3.1
Requests teacher help/feedback	1.4	0.6	1.1	1.1
Organizes materials	2.5	4.0	0.9	0.5
Total on task	64.1	85.9	72.1	72.9
Off task				
Not attending	26.7	7.0	26.2	11.7
Attending non-task teacher talk	2.7	3.7	1.1	9.5
Peer interaction	6.5	3.5	0.7	5.8
Total off task	35.9	14.2	28.0	27.0

Although they were in the same class they showed quite different patterns of involvement during the observations. In language Jonathan was on task more than Timothy, the great majority of that time being spent on individual work. Timothy spent more time attending to the teacher and in interacting with peers about his work. This tendency to interact more also shows up in non-task talk. As will be seen later the proportion of off-task behaviour in this class was the highest of all the special school classes, the greatest part of which was in the not attending category. A great deal of this was passive, e.g. staring into space, but much of Jonathan's off-task behaviour in language was due to physical disruption, a consequence of his reaction to being thumped in the back.

Timothy's involvement was much higher in his maths work, and was higher than Jonathan's. The main difference between the two was in the pattern of off-task behaviour, where Jonathan talked to his peers more and was also drawn off task listening to the teacher talking about non-work issues.

Transfer

Jonathan and Timothy both transferred at the age of 14 into the fourth years of two very different comprehensive schools.

Of all the children studied Jonathan had the most opportunity to gain experience of the new school before the actual transfer. However, the news of his transfer into the ordinary school 'came out of the blue' for his prospective special needs teacher, and there had been no liaison at all between teachers in the special and ordinary schools. Jonathan had had an interview to discuss the feasibility of his attending the school and it was this, it seems, that set the ball rolling in terms of the effort made to integrate him into the system. The meeting was attended by the head teacher, the deputy head, an officer from the LEA education department, Jonathan and his mother. The special needs teacher was aware that this meeting had been something of an ordeal for Jonathan, as it had been very formal and he had performed poorly. Despite his poor performance it was agreed that Jonathan should be given a trial at the school and also that he should attend the school for one week before the beginning of term to give him an opportunity to become acclimatized to it. It seemed that the level of concern at the thought of receiving a child from a special school who was obviously very weak academically was such that the school did everything in its power to ensure that the consequences were not catastrophic for either the child or itself. Thus Jonathan attended the school for one week in July. The school found him a uniform and he went on the first year's school trip. It gave the remedial teacher an opportunity to do some testing and enabled her to get to know Jonathan and sort out a timetable that he could cope with. She sought agreement from other staff about placing Jonathan in their sets and took care only to approach those she thought would be willing, following her instincts in this respect. All was discussed individually and negotiated, so that anyone unwilling to teach him was either not approached or had the opportunity to refuse. The teacher felt that there was no point in thrusting Jonathan on staff and telling them to cope, as she believed that if they did not want to then they would not.

The general system in Jonathan's new school was that children entering the first year were placed, according to the recommendations made by their primary school teachers and their performance in standardized tests, into one of four groups, A, B, C or remedial. Those placed in the remedial group generally had reading ages approximately two years below their chronological age and showed poor concept development in maths, and usually numbered about ten. They were kept as a separate class for intensive help during their first year. Alongside this, children within the mainstream who experienced difficulties in maths or English or both were withdrawn for up to six hours of maths and eight hours of English according to their needs. In the second year the special class was disbanded and the children were placed in mainstream with provision continuing as a less intensive form of withdrawal. This continued into the third year. In the fourth year a special option for those with learning difficulties was provided—supplementary English and maths. This included the type of basic English and maths skills that pupils would find useful to have at work. Before Christmas in the final year, all completed a basic AEB exam in arithmetic, English and life-skills to provide those leaving school at Easter with the opportunity to gain a qualification. The SEN teacher felt the results of the course had been good. All children with learning difficulties leaving school in the previous two years had achieved this certificate. An additional development within the authority that the teacher thought useful was a proficiency in English examination that was being piloted. She also thought that some new modules might be introduced for those who were having difficulties with the CSE courses. NEB modular units were suggested as being the possible replacements.

Jonathan entered at the options stage. As indicated above Jonathan's teacher thought carefully about his ability to cope in each subject, but as a consequence his timetable was very restricted and heavily geared towards maths and language. These two subjects took up nearly thirteen hours of his normal week, well over 50 per cent of the timetable. The only other subjects available to him were art, PE, games, woodwork, housecraft and care.

In complete contrast Timothy had no contact whatsoever with the new school before transfer. No visit was arranged and no liaison took place between teachers. His English teacher said that Timothy had 'just appeared'. The general provision for children with special educational needs was weak at the school, a situation exacerbated by the absence of the head of the remedial department, due to a nervous breakdown. The basic system was that special provision, in the form of a remedial class, was only available in the first two years. Thereafter the children were placed in mainstream groups taught in the normal way by subject specialists. Thus, as the teachers argued, the ground originally gained was largely lost through a total lack of support for the weakest children after year two. No formal links existed between departments for liaison, and no school policy existed concerning how to cater for children with learning difficulties. It was, as one teacher said, a case of 'mend and make do'. The lack of policy within the school mirrored the lack of policy in the LEA. Children were being transferred from special schools but no support was being offered of any kind.

Timothy therefore entered a school that provided no specific support for him, with few options open to him. His secondary school curriculum was, in addition to language and maths, limited to seven subjects: art, games, PE, humanities, general science, woodwork and vehicle maintenance. Language and maths activities took up over a third of the timetable. The teachers in the ordinary school were questioned about their approaches and about what flexibility existed to cater for individual needs. Timothy's English teacher said that he had not made any changes to his basic methods to deal explicitly with Timothy. His approach was literature-based and he chose books that were more suited to lower ability readers. His style was described as being 'less formal' and involving much drama, reading and discussion. 'I bought a lot of books which are more suited to kids who find difficulty with reading. There are always the very, very popular ones and no matter how good or bad their reading kids in this school love to read *Kes* still and you read it with them, of course. And a lot of *Topliners* and such things, with a simple approach on modern classics and so on with the reading specifically designed for low ability teenage readers and they enjoy that.... I tend not to go for a formal approach for English with this type of group.'

In contrast, Timothy's maths teacher said he adapted his material and methods when necessary to cater specifically for Timothy's needs. 'If Timothy had problems then I would suggest an alternative for him.' He also adapted work for one other pupil in his group who had quite severe difficulties. An individualized approach for the whole class using the Kent Maths Scheme had been considered, but had not been implemented. At the time of interviewing they were working on producing a suitable scheme. 'We're working on it, let's put it that way. The person who was originally in charge of it has gone on a course and hopefully he'll come back with all sorts of original ideas.... My original scheme was the scheme of a person who had taught people O levels and CSEs and it was a watered down version of the CSE syllabus. Obviously with Cockcroft it had to change and I think we will produce a very good syllabus for these people. It has to be something quite different as opposed to doing simple examples of Pythagoras' theorem. Hopefully it will be something more meaningful to them.'

In English and maths Jonathan found himself in very small groups, from eight children upwards. His special needs teacher used a variety of methods and schemes. In language she had used *Language Through Experience* for the first time and found the course useful. Jonathan, for example, was interested in the Beatles and in fishing and his teacher used these topics as a base to work from. Having worked in adult literacy for some years, she also used the materials and experience she had gleaned there.

Jonathan's mainstream English teacher also tried to base work on the children's experience and to use a variety of methods depending on the content of work. However, as all within the group except Jonathan were following an examination syllabus, this tended to act as a constraint. She thought that he tended to be pushed to one side as a result, but she had not changed her methods in any way to deal with that problem. On such occasions Jonathan simply had to wait for attention. His supplementary English teacher had not produced an individual programme for Jonathan as her contact with him was minimal. However, she had adapted her approach so that his learning difficulties were not compounded by technical difficulties. For example, she did not ask the group (of 13 low attaining fourth years) to do copying from the blackboard. Jonathan also did some maths work with his special needs teacher, working from the *Headway* scheme, and was a member of a CSE maths group. The maths teacher did not think that Jonathan was capable of taking the examination, but it was school policy not to label anyone 'non-exam'. The teacher felt that he coped reasonably well although he worked considerably more slowly than the rest despite the fact that as a group they were disruptive. Reflecting this, the teacher said of Jonathan: 'He usually sits on his own and I think he realizes that the rest of these lot are idiots.'

Ordinary School

Curriculum

Mathematics Despite the maths teacher's claims, the nature of the maths that Timothy experienced differed greatly from that with which he was familiar. Although work on the four rules continued, usually in the context of another area, the majority of the work sampled concentrated on shape, area and measurement. This work included symmetry, co-ordinates, scale, length and, after preliminary work on covering space, work on areas of shapes beginning with triangles. Timothy appeared to find this work difficult, and this was confirmed in his end of year examinations, where he gained a mark of 16 per cent, effort B+. Tried hard without much success.

From Jonathan's work sample the curriculum covered appeared to be constricted despite the large amount of time devoted to it. Much work was done on the four rules up to thousands through the area of money. Money problems included the payment of bills and working out amounts to pay from rates and rateable values. General work on the four rules also occurred in the area of time, e.g. working on timetables. There was evidence of work on the 24 hour clock and on measurement, beginning with people.

Language An analysis of the work sampled from Timothy is shown in Table 4.4.

Table 4.4. *Timothy's language work.*

Comprehension	Many such tasks culled from various sources: commercial cards, work cards, poems
Story writing	Included 'My biggest lie', 'Lost in the desert', 'My idea of a holiday'
Project	e.g. motorbikes
Grammar	Capitals, punctuation

The general standard of his work was poor. His spelling was very poor but no efforts appeared to have been made to improve it. His stories were often no more than lists of points, and much of his project writing was simply copied from newspaper reports or books. When he did write a story of some length it was clear that he had only rudimentary knowledge of grammar. Capitals did not follow full stops, and the stories were a series of events of the 'and then' type. Despite this the teacher's comments on his work were of little value. A typical comment at the end of a story with the features listed above would be a tick and 'you need to look at each sentence'.

Jonathan's language experience showed many commonalities (Table 4.5).

Table 4.5. *Jonathan's language work.*

Grammar	Several exercises on alphabetical order
Concepts: description and sorting	Describing/making sentences around concepts, e.g. money, food; sorting concepts into categories
Factual writing	Letter writing; letters of complaint; form filling
Poetry	Copying poems, e.g. Spike Milligan

Examination of samples of work indicates Jonathan's continuing difficulties with grammar. Capital letters were used almost randomly and not always after a full stop. Spelling errors were fairly common and some basic words in letter writing were portrayed incorrectly, e.g. faith fully instead of faithfully. The teacher's reaction to these difficulties appeared to be to ignore them completely. Most were signified with a tick, and only a tick. None was graced with a word of comment.

Task involvement (see Table 4.6)

Task involvement was much higher in the ordinary school although the figures are likely to be over-optimistic. For example, observations were not undertaken during transition periods, during which much time is wasted, and whenever there was a difficulty in inferring the behavioural intent, the child was given the benefit of the doubt. For example, much more time was spent staring into space in the ordinary school. Was the child thinking or totally switched off through boredom? Whenever there was doubt in the observer's mind it was categorized as the former.

The pattern of involvement is quite different from that in the special school, notably the marked increase in the amount of time spent attending to the teacher. This clearly reflects the increased prevalence of didactic teaching and the teacher-centred approach, particularly in Jonathan's school, which, incidentally, was an ex-grammar school. There is also an indication that involvement tended to fall off in the sessions observed in the summer term. This is particularly true in Jonathan's language work, where nearly half of his time was spent not attending. This was not a case of disruptive behaviour: he simply showed an almost total lack of interest in his work. Jonathan's special school teacher had commented that Jonathan often needed a steam roller to get him going and it seems that initial motivation to do well may have waned by the third term.

Appropriateness

Increasing involvement in tasks is of course of little value if the work set is not appropriate. Data on appropriateness were collected in maths and language activities in the same way as reported by Bennett *et al.* (1987). Time limited these observations to approximately eight tasks per child, and so the trends should only be regarded as suggestive.

In language work there was evidence to suggest that more tasks were set in the ordinary school that were too difficult for Jonathan and Timothy than in the special school. The main problem appeared to be that many set tasks failed to take adequate account of their weaknesses in that area. For example, Timothy was set a fact-finding task requiring the identification of the capital cities, language and currency of different countries. Timothy understood the requirements but could not carry the task out because his knowledge of the alphabet was so tenuous that he could not use an encyclopaedia. The teacher told him that he should learn the alphabet. Jonathan had similar difficulties in a task that demanded group discussion of an abstract. He was unable to read the abstract and could only listen to the discussion without being able to participate himself.

Table 4.6. *Task involvement in maths and language: ordinary school. Figures are percentage of time spent on each activity.*

	Timothy				Jonathan			
	Ordinary I		Ordinary III		Ordinary I		Ordinary III	
	Language	Maths	Language	Maths	Language	Maths	Language	Maths
On task								
Individual work	53.2	65.0	33.9	53.5	47.3	56.9	4.6	38.9
Attending to teacher	29.7	31.4	9.0	35.4	43.7	32.0	47.3	45.3
Peer interaction	8.4	2.3	39.3	2.1	2.4	4.6	0.4	1.9
Requests teacher help/feedback	0.5	0.6	1.5	2.4	1.9	1.1	0.3	2.2
Organizes materials	2.0	—	4.8	1.1	1.4	1.3	1.1	5.7
Total on task	93.8	99.3	88.5	94.5	96.7	95.9	53.7	94.0
Off task								
Not attending	4.1	0.2	4.5	5.4	1.5	1.7	45.5	6.0
Attending non-task teacher talk	0.9	0.1	1.2	—	0.6	2.3	0.7	—
Peer interaction	1.3	0.4	5.8	—	1.3	—	—	—
Total off task	6.3	0.7	11.5	5.4	3.4	4.0	46.2	6.0

In mathematics the pattern in special school was for the tasks to be familiar and relatively easy. In the ordinary school they were not familiar and tended to be more difficult, but not always too difficult. There were also examples of the ordinary school teacher reorganizing an overestimate and reacting accordingly. For example, Timothy was set work on the area of parallelograms, about which he was totally confused. The teacher, recognizing this, dropped the demand to area of squares, which Timothy was able to do.

Summary

The two boys had very different experiences of transfer. There was no liaison in either case, but Jonathan's school, faced with a different kind of being from that they were used to, made special arrangements that ironically led to a very narrow curriculum heavily dominated by maths and language.

Jonathan and Timothy experienced very different curriculum on either side of the transfer. There was a marked discontinuity in maths, where much of the work was new, unfamiliar and often too difficult for them, although some efforts were made to modify task demand. The content was more familiar in language but insufficient attention was paid to the skills, or lack of them, that Jonathan and Timothy entered with. Similarly, teacher comments on completed work were not helpful or constructive.

The boys' involvement was higher in the ordinary school, a response partly to the different teaching approaches adopted, and partly to their eagerness to please in the first term. There was an indication that work involvement had fallen away by the third term.

SARAH AND PETER

Sarah and Peter were in the same special school class but transferred into the first year of different comprehensive schools at the age of 11.

Special school

Curriculum

There were, as might be expected, many common elements in these children's curriculum. Their experiences in mathematics are shown in Table 4.7.

Sarah was in the 'top group' in maths and this appears to be represented by additional work on division problems, shape and measurement. The teacher worked from several sources, including *Hey Mathematics*, *Numbers and Words* and *Alpha and Beta*. Sarah appeared to be competent in most of the areas covered but the teacher pointed out that she had problems in carrying figures when multiplying and dividing, and needed concrete aids for certain operations. Although she was able to compute in the four rules she lacked basic understanding to apply the rules in relevant situations. The teacher stressed that Sarah needed to consolidate new concepts with practice, and that structured methods were needed, including work on tables.

Table 4.7. *Maths curriculum: special school.*

		Sarah	Peter
Addition	Computation	HTU	HTU
	Problems	TU	TU
Subtraction	Computation	HTU	HTU
	Problems	TU	TU
Multiplication	Computation	HTU to × 5	HTU × U
	Problems	HTU to × 5	TU
Division	Computation	HTU to ÷ 5	HTU ÷ 5
	Problems	HTU to ÷ 5	—
Fractions		Addition of ½	½, ⅓
Money		Counting, giving change	Change, add to £1
Time		To 5 minutes	To 5 minutes
Shape		Identification of	
Measurement		Hand spans/ruler in cms	

According to the teacher Peter was keen and enthusiastic, being able to work accurately and grasp new concepts quickly. She was confident in Peter's ability to work the four rules in hundreds, tens and units with carrying. He could tell the time and his work on money was good. He knew several tables, those up to 5, and 10 and 11.

Language The samples of work analysed for Sarah and Peter showed some considerable commonalities. Their work could be classified into seven basic categories, as follows:

1. Comprehension; using reading laboratory; sentence completion.
2. Phonics; range of phonic skills including blends.
3. Grammar; sentence construction; re-phrasing of questions; answering in full sentences; dictation.
4. Story writing; including letter writing.
5. Factual writing; including diary.
6. Reading; Ginn scheme.
7. Handwriting; letter formation.

In her early written work Sarah tended to list events rather than to write extended sentences and there were some problems with punctuation. Nevertheless, Sarah was using joined letters and her writing was neat and well spaced. By the time of transfer her teacher reported that her major strength was her creative writing; that her sentence construction was excellent, her phonic skills good and her spelling quite good. However, her general vocabulary needed expanding. She transferred with a reading age of 8½.

In his last months in the special school Peter, like Sarah, had been exposed to a variety of schemes in reading and language work. The Ginn reading scheme had been adopted for reading, but for language work the tasks came from Reading Laboratories, Oxford Workbooks, Tansley *Sound Sense* and teacher made worksheets. During this period Peter was having difficulty writing more than short sentences, and his spelling was generally poor. The teacher took note of these errors and wrote the correct word above the misspellings, to be copied out three times. Peter's handwriting was generally neat and the words were well spaced.

In the report from the special to the ordinary school Peter's reading age was given as 8 years, and his spelling age as 6 months less than that. It was reported that he had good phonic ability and that his work in creative writing, sentence construction and punctuation were good. He did, of course, need additional work on spelling and his general vocabulary needed extending.

Task involvement

Table 4.8 shows the extent and type of involvement for both children.

Table 4.8. *Task involvement: special school. Figures are percentage of time spent on each activity.*

	Sarah		Peter	
	Language	Maths	Language	Maths
On task				
Individual work	42.9	29.0	59.9	49.8
Attending to teacher	49.2	56.0	24.1	11.2
Peer interaction	0.5	2.3	6.2	4.6
Requests teacher help/feedback	0.7	4.8	1.4	3.1
Organizes materials	0.2	—	0.3	3.9
Total on task	93.5	92.1	91.9	72.6
Off task				
Not attending	2.0	4.0	4.0	27.4
Attending non-task teacher talk	3.4	3.3	3.4	—
Peer interaction	1.0	0.8	0.7	—
Total off task	6.4	8.1	8.1	27.4

We have demonstrated in earlier studies (e.g. Bennett *et al.*, 1980) that within-class differences in patterns of involvement can be large. This is shown in Table 4.8, where Sarah's profile in language and mathematics is quite different from Peter's. In language Sarah spends twice as much time attending to teacher and much less time interacting with peers even though the overall involvement rates are not dissimilar. The contrasts in maths are even more stark. Here too Sarah attends to substantially more teacher input, whereas Peter's profile is more typical of maths, being focused on individual work. Classroom organization issues are also brought to the fore in Peter's non-attending profile. The 27 per cent not attending figure was, in large part, teacher induced. Peter was placed in a queue awaiting teacher attention for much of one of the lessons observed.

Transfer

In each case of children transferring into the first year of secondary school the level of contact that took place between the special and ordinary schools, particularly preceding transfer, was far greater than that which took place when children transferred into the fourth year. Children entering the first year slotted into an established structure while the others did not.

The system of liaison between Sarah's and Peter's special school and the ordinary schools was particularly successful because the special school teacher, being particularly concerned about the success of integrated children, had initiated the contacts. This positive philosophy was reflected in the comments of the head of the remedial department in the school to which Sarah transferred, who stated his belief that the children from that special school generally integrated successfully, and that the stance of the special school was very helpful. The head teacher of the special school had visited the secondary school, and the head of the remedial department had visited the special school. The special school was kept informed of the transferred children's progress through copies of school reports, examination results and the like.

Liaison with Peter's school was also good. The head of the first year had visited the special school, and the head of the special school had visited the ordinary school. In addition Peter had visited the school in July with all the other children transferring at 11. The only hiccup was that Peter's records did not arrive until a month after transfer.

A banding system operated in the first three years in Sarah's school. Children were placed within this, or in the remedial form that ran alongside it, according to their results in a battery of tests given to all first years, to assess their levels of competence in basic skills, a fortnight after they entered the school. The remedial group was taught as a class and was exposed to all subject teachers, as were other forms. The only significant difference was that they were given supplementary English lessons. For these lessons the class was split into two and provided with two specialist remedial teachers, so that the tuition could be more intensive. The form teacher of the first year special needs group thought that children with special needs were well catered for within the school. 'I think that in terms of provision for children with special needs they are very comfortably catered for and this school is aware of the problems and it's our aim to ensure a comfortable, happy school life and educational attainment.' However, the type of provision that was made within the school was the subject of thought if not of debate. An HMI who had visited the school had suggested that children within the remedial group were being over-protected. The head teacher was considering the possibility of introducing a withdrawal system.

In Peter's school thought was being given to the possibility of introducing a system of in-class support for children in mixed ability classes. This was the result, it seemed, of a teacher who, having attended a course, had come back into school with new ideas about how provision might be organized. However, the small group within the special needs department who were contemplating the possibility of change were aware that such a venture would be dependent on a number of factors, such as timetabling, the bugbear of the secondary system, and staff commitment. At that time the idea had been discussed only within the special needs department. Currently, from an intake of more than 200, 28 children were placed in a remedial group, which was split into two for all subject teaching. All other children were placed in mixed ability classes. Remedial provision was made in this way until the third year. After that children were extracted where there was a need.

Sarah's curriculum in the first year was broader than Peter's. They experienced in common art, drama, English, French, maths, music, PE and science. Sarah studied geography and history separately while Peter studied social studies. In addition Sarah spent time in domestic science and life skills. The amount of time devoted to subjects also varied widely. In English, for example, Sarah was timetabled for five hours per week compared to Peter's three and a quarter hours. On the other hand, Peter was timetabled for four and a half hours of mathematics, half an hour more than Sarah.

Ordinary school

Curriculum

Mathematics Sarah's work in maths was guided by *Headway Maths* but little headway was in fact made. Sarah was given work in addition and subtraction that was below her competence, and no work on division was covered. Some extension work was carried out in multiplication where she was introduced to multiplying from ×6 to ×9. No work on fractions was attempted, and the work on time (carried out in English lessons) did not extend that in the special school. New work was undertaken in shapes and graphs. The work on shapes introduced Sarah to parallel and perpendicular lines and the recognition of complex shapes, such as irregular quadrilaterals and trapeziums. In graph work simple bar charts and pictographs were taught with simple numbers.

From the facsimiles of Sarah's work provided by the teacher she appeared to have little difficulty, which is perhaps not surprising given the large amount of revision work apparent in the first term.

The SMP mathematics scheme had very recently been introduced into Peter's school. The special needs teacher was very pleased with it since it allowed children to work at their own pace, 'and they're graded so they can get a bit of everything at a very simple level, and that's consolidated before they move on to the next thing'. Unfortunately, the sample of Peter's work did not portray much excitement. There was a good deal of replication of work on the four rules followed by a heavy concentration on fractions and decimals before introductory algebra of the type $2a + 5a + 9a =$

Language Sarah's class teacher said that she tried to use a variety of approaches and a combination of activities with the class, from individual work to group projects. They also read aloud and had class discussions on, for example, news items. In contrast, Sarah's further English teacher used specific schemes, particularly *Sound Sense* and Oxford worksheets. The sampled work broke down as follows:

1. Comprehension; exercises from textbook.
2. Story writing; many examples: 'My family', 'A witch', 'If I had a lot of money', etc.
3. Factual writing, e.g. on characters in *Oliver Twist*.

4.   Letter writing, e.g. to classmate who was ill.
5.   Grammar; question marks, use of time, months of year and seasons, capital letters.
6.   Reading; Ginn.

Sarah's work was generally good, most of it being graded in the B category. She did, however, have difficulty with spelling but the way in which the teacher reacted to this was the opposite of that of Timothy's and Jonathan's teacher. Sarah's teacher appeared to have very clear ideas about the value of comments. Each spelling error was identified and each had to be written out three times. In addition to the comments, both on the text and on associated drawings, and the demands for corrections, the teacher graded each piece of work. The appearance of the work was akin to that in primary schools. Stories were often illustrated, and some group story writing was attempted.

Peter's teacher said that the class usually worked individually so that they could work at their own pace. Although there was a basic first year syllabus that was adhered to it was adapted to children's needs. The sample of work provided was grouped as follows:

1.   Comprehension, e.g. 'On a desert island', 'Bright eyes'.
2.   Story writing, e.g. 'The escape'.
3.   Factual writing, e.g. Grace Darling.
4.   Grammar; Sentences and capital letters; exercises on tenses, adjectives, capitals.
5.   Phonics; crosswords emphasizing 'sh', 'ch'; exercises on 'aw' and 'oo' sounds.

In contrast to Sarah's experiences Peter's curriculum had a much greater emphasis on grammar and phonics. In general Peter's work was quite good. His grammar was adequate and although there were spelling errors these were not extensive. The teacher's reaction to them differed markedly from that of Sarah's teacher. The misspellings were picked out by writing the correct spellings over the top of the offending word, but there was no demand from the teacher for Peter to do anything about it. The teacher's comments were typically exceedingly brief, one of the longest being 'a good try'.

Task involvement (see Table 4.9)

The levels of involvement for both Sarah and Peter were very high, partly for reasons outlined earlier. However, it should be borne in mind that their on-task behaviour was also high in the special school, except for Peter's enforced queuing in maths. The patterns in the ordinary school for both children are very similar, with the exception of the increased co-operative group work element in Sarah's English, manifested in the high peer interaction category.

Appropriateness

Task involvement may have been similar, but what of the appropriateness of the work given? In Peter's case in mathematics there appeared to be little difference. Approximately one-third of the tasks demanded were too hard, one-third too easy and one-third matched. In Sarah's case two-thirds of the tasks in the ordinary school were

Table 4.9. *Task involvement: ordinary school. Figures are percentage of time spent on each activity.*

	Sarah				Peter			
	Ordinary I		Ordinary III		Ordinary I		Ordinary III	
	Language	Maths	Language	Maths	Language	Maths	Language	Maths
On task								
Individual work	74.6	76.4	19.9	47.1	54.5	69.0	56.3	63.6
Attending to teacher	19.6	20.4	44.0	41.7	38.2	27.4	28.3	23.2
Peer interaction	0.8	1.0	22.7	1.2	0.8	0.7	0.3	6.8
Requests teacher help/feedback	1.3	0.9	1.6	1.9	0.9	0.1	8.3	0.7
Organizes materials	0.6	0.9	5.1	6.5	2.8	0.4	1.7	3.2
Total on task	96.9	99.6	92.3	98.4	97.2	97.6	94.9	97.5
Off task								
Not attending	1.4	0.1	4.9	1.5	2.7	2.0	5.1	1.8
Attending non-task teacher talk	1.1	0.3	1.9	—	—	0.2	—	—
Peer interaction	0.4	—	—	0.2	—	0.1	—	0.7
Total off task	2.9	0.4	6.8	1.7	2.7	2.3	5.1	2.5

matched and one-third were too easy. It should be recalled that these observations took place in the first term, and the too easy tasks tended to be revision work. In these cases it could be argued that such tasks, even if too easy, are necessary for diagnostic purposes.

As with maths, Peter's language tasks were similarly matched on either side of transfer: two-thirds were appropriate and one-third too difficult. Peter experienced most problems with lessons on spelling that were beyond his capabilities. Sarah, on the other hand, tended to be underestimated more. Fifty per cent of her tasks in both schools were appropriate and 50 per cent too easy. Tasks that were too easy included a lesson where the children simply copied out an essay written in a previous lesson.

Summary

Sarah and Peter transferred from the same special school to different secondary schools. Transfer appeared to be a smooth process, aided, in large part, by the special school teacher who had instigated and developed a successful liaison system.

Each child entered a remedial class but they experienced different curricula in terms of both width and content. Despite this a comparison of the curriculum on either side of transfer leads to the same conclusion for both maths and language work, i.e. evidence of continuity but little extension. There appeared to be an over-concentration on revision work in the first term, which led at times to the tasks underestimating the children, particularly Sarah. The extent of their involvement in the work provided varied little across transfer or across terms.

ANNA

Special school

Curriculum

Anna transferred at the age of 11 to her local comprehensive school. Before this she had experienced a transfer-back programme in maths and language work. Table 4.10 sketches out her maths programme in the special school.

This programme was based around *Peak Maths* books 4 and 5. It can be seen from the table that the work assumed competence in the four rules. The focus was on fractions and decimals, money, time and measurement. Computation and problem-solving were carried out within the context of these topics. For example, in changing fractions to decimals Anna had to carry out multiplication in HTU in such sums as $342\frac{3}{10}$. Subtraction in problem form was required in money, in tackling such questions as 'I borrowed £1200 from the bank to pay for a garage. The garage cost £2074 to build. How much more money did I need?' Despite all this effort the teacher claimed that maths was Anna's weakest link.

Anna also followed a transfer-back programme in language work. The cover was extensive, as the following list indicates.

1.   Comprehension; 'Spaceships', 'the Royal Family'; exercises from *Sound Sense*.
2.   Story writing; 'Sally the seagull', 'My Easter holidays'.

Table 4.10. *Maths curriculum: special school.*

Addition	Computation	THTU
	Problems	—
Subtraction	Computation	—
	Problems	—
Multiplication	Computation	—
	Problems	—
Division	Computation	HTU ÷ U
	Problems	—
Fractions		½ to ¹⁄₁₀, multi. ⅛ of 32
Decimals		Conversion of fractions to decimals and vice versa
Money		± TU, problems to THTU
Time		To 5 minutes, problems
Measurement		Metric conversion, maps, scale (cm)

3. Grammar; adjectives, consonant blends, sentence construction, alphabetical order.
4. Phonics; long vowel sounds, 'ing' endings, 'ar' sounds.
5. Spelling; Tansley spelling cards.
6. Handwriting.

The cover was of more formal aspects of language, on the assumption that these were what would be required in the ordinary school. The teacher noted that Anna was able to work unaided, that her reading was very good and that her comprehension was also good. Her punctuation needed extra work.

Task involvement

Anna's work involvement was high, averaging over 90 per cent, as Table 4.11 shows. It can be seen from this that the vast majority of Anna's work was individual, with very little contact with teacher or peers in either subject.

Transfer

Anna moved from a well-organized special school into a comprehensive school that appeared to have given little thought to provision for remedial children. Indeed the head of the remedial department said that they 'tended to be left to the bottom of the pile'. The school was over-subscribed and teachers' timetables were filled up by giving them remedial groups.

The remedial class tended to be small, about fifteen children, and catered for slow learners and those with behavioural or adjustment problems. The class followed the same timetable as all other children and only a slightly modified curriculum. The only

Table 4.11. *Task involvement: ordinary school. Figures are percentages of time spent on each activity*

	Language	Maths
On task		
Individual work	75.3	84.8
Attending to teacher	15.2	5.7
Peer interaction	0.3	0.3
Requests teacher help/feedback	0.7	2.5
Organizes materials	—	2.5
Total on task	91.5	95.8
Off task		
Not attending	1.1	4.2
Attending non-task teacher talk	2.4	—
Peer interaction	5.0	—
Total off task	8.5	4.2

difference was that chemistry and French were replaced by extra maths and English. The remedial head was not happy with this, arguing that 'the problem is that some people obviously don't relate to these children very well and don't want to teach them and are not very interested'. He was attempting to overcome this problem by discussing the possibility of one teacher within each department taking responsibility for remedial children.

Within the current system there was no provision for children within mainstream classes in the school. However, this was likely to change following the appointment of a teacher to take responsibility for all children with special educational needs in the school irrespective of placement. The remedial teacher hoped that this would change thinking and practice in the school: 'It'll end, I think, the concept that "if you get a child with a problem, put them in the remedial department. Because it's a small group they'll be able to do something." That isn't the case, it's not necessary in a lot of cases, it's not the answer in a lot of cases. It holds back more than it pushes on children in that situation. The answer is to be able to deal with them in the class in which they belong and we are working towards that.'

A further difficulty identified by Anna's teacher was that the children were not taught as a group for every subject, but were sometimes mixed with other classes for administrative reasons. There were twelve children in Anna's class and they remained as a group except for practical subjects like domestic science and needlework. This was an administrative decision rather than an educational one: 'It has to be done. All the first years are on practical subjects at the same time and they have to divide neatly into sets of 20 so we get the children in the R form being moved in to make up the 20. If the class, say, has eighteen boys doing woodwork, two of my boys might then be taken off to make up the 20, so it doesn't benefit them because they are working with children who are far more skilled, far more articulate and everything that they aren't. But also they are divided, they are not even kept together as a set very often and staff who teach them say that there's very little they can do for them.'

A similar lack of thought had been given to liaison. No visits to or from the ordinary school had been made, and the remedial teacher had not been given any information about Anna and her needs, although he thought this was more likely to be a breakdown in communication within his school than between the schools. 'The headmaster of [the special school] may well have contacted our headmaster but it certainly hasn't filtered through. He did know we were going to get this girl but he either didn't know or couldn't explain what her specific problems were.'

When teachers were interviewed about their teaching approaches and schemes it became apparent that some thought had been given by the English teacher, but that maths had suffered from staffing problems. The methods used by the English teacher were designed to cater for children with special needs. He gave each child a series of tasks that they were to complete within the week, which enabled him to respond to each child's abilities and levels of performance individually, perhaps giving one child only one work card to do and another three. These could be completed in any order. Moreover, he attempted to provide the children with more individual attention by using enthusiastic sixth formers in the school as helpers. On occasions they would extract a small group of children to work on a particular problem, such as their spelling. In reading a similar flexible but structured system operated. 'What I do is provide a certain number of books in the class on a sort of library basis. These are books that children can opt for, they can take and do what they like with them and they can pick and choose as they feel. I don't guide them to do that. What I do is I keep a number of schemes separate and then children that have the special problems I say to them, "well, you can have whatever reading book you like, but when you come to me we will use this particular scheme", and these are things like *Sound Sense* and *Wide Range Readers*. With particularly difficult cases things like *Nippers*, which is quite an old one but very nice, the *Griffin Pirates* and that sort of thing.'

Mathematics had proved to be problematic in that year, as Anna's special needs teacher explained. 'We've had a particular problem in maths this year, a staffing problem. They've had about four or five different teachers. They follow the school syllabus as far as possible, but it's not really a question of here is a book or particular scheme. Certainly not an SMP or KMP or any of the maths projects. They use an appropriate text book for whatever activity they are doing. I think some of them at times might even still be using *Beta* books, but that wouldn't be a rigid scheme.'

Ordinary school

Curriculum

Anna's maths curriculum in the ordinary school is shown in Table 4.12. As was indicated above, the staffing of maths was fragmented and no scheme guided the work. However, judged from the sample of work collected, competence was assumed in the four rules, although those were most often carried out in the context of money. The work that Anna was presented with did little other than provide revision of content previously covered, with the exception of some introductory geometry.

The work in language was as follows:

1. Comprehension; work cards (*Stride Ahead*); synonyms; word meanings; SRA cards, e.g. 'The Playful King'.
2. Story writing; 'An adventure with my pet'.

Table 4.12. *Mathematics curriculum: ordinary school.*

Addition	Computation	HTU
	Problems	—
Subtraction	Computation	HTU
	Problems	—
Multiplication	Computation	HTU × U
	Problems	—
Division	Computation	HTU ÷ U
	Problems	—
Fractions		½ to $\frac{1}{10}$, 1/5 of 45, LCM
Decimals		± TU
Money		HTU (÷×+−) TU
Measurement		Co-ordinates (cm)
Geometry		Arcs, angles

3. Grammar; exercises on verbs, collective nouns, tenses, sentence construction; alphabetical order.
4. Spelling
5. Factual writing, e.g. 'Myself'.

   Despite the earlier description of the teacher's teaching approach, the reality was a marked emphasis on grammar and comprehension, with very little writing. Anna performed well on these tasks since they were very similar in type to the tasks in her transfer-back programme. Anna gained either a comment of 'very good' or a grade A. In spelling the teacher identified each error and required five copies of each word. The comments were generally not extensive but were positive in tone, and occasionally directed Anna's attention to a specific point, e.g. that capital letters needed to be bigger.

Task involvement

It can be seen from Table 4.13 that Anna's involvement continued to be high in the ordinary school, although there is evidence of a slight fall-off in the third term. The pattern of involvement is quite different, however, since, as with Jonathan and Timothy, the impact of a more didactic, teacher-centred approach is quite clear in the increased proportion of time spent attending to teacher. The increased non-attendance in the third term was passive, indicating lack of interest rather than behavioural difficulties.

Appropriateness

The appropriateness of the work observed was generally good in both maths and language activities in the special and ordinary schools. The work in maths in the

Table 4.13. *Task involvement: ordinary school. Figures are percentages of time spent on each activity.*

	Ordinary I		Ordinary III	
	Language	Maths	Language	Maths
On task				
Individual work	66.6	69.3	42.8	60.6
Attending to teacher	25.8	18.2	25.3	21.9
Peer interaction	0.4	2.5	0.5	1.2
Requests teacher help/feedback	1.4	4.5	1.5	2.5
Organizes materials	1.2	0.2	15.3	2.5
Total on task	95.4	94.7	85.4	88.7
Off task				
Not attending	3.4	2.3	13.3	9.6
Attending non-task teacher talk	0.5	2.0	1.0	0.7
Peer interaction	0.7	1.0	0.1	0.9
Total off task	4.6	5.3	14.4	11.2

ordinary school tended to be new, e.g. angles, intersections, etc., but was generally matched to Anna's capabilities. The instances where it was too difficult tended to be for procedural rather than for academic reasons. For example, in one task she was required to draw an angle of 68° ensuring that AB = 12 cm and CA = 13 cm. Anna understood what to do but was frustrated in her attempt because she could not use the protractor correctly.

Summary

Anna transferred from a highly organized special school to a comprehensive school that was lacking in both organization for and interest in children with special educational needs. Liaison was poor and there was no indication that continuity of curriculum had been planned for. In reality the curriculum offered heavily overlapped that studied by Anna in her transfer-back programme. It is likely, therefore, that the tasks observed for appropriateness were an unrepresentative sample, since most were in the area of geometry, the only new area for Anna in maths.

The extent of her work involvement was similar on either side of transfer but showed a slight tendency to fade by the third term.

Chapter 5

The Integration Process.
III: Academic and Social
Integration—Pupil and Teacher
Perspectives

In Chapter 4 we considered the process of transfer. In this chapter we consider the effects of that process. We argue that the most important effects are the extent to which the children were successfully integrated, both academically and socially. The data relevant to these issues were collected by extensive interviews with the pupils, their teachers and their parents. In this chapter the view from inside the school is the focus, and the parental perspective is dealt with in the next chapter.

ACADEMIC INTEGRATION

Jonathan and Timothy

It will be recalled that these two boys transferred from the same special school to different comprehensive schools at the age of 14. Teachers in the latter schools described them both as having good attitudes to school, although in Timothy's case the teacher qualified this to 'on surface appearance'. Timothy appeared to work well in class but the teacher was no doubt influenced by his increasing absences from school, and his very poor examination results.

Despite his reasonable attitude to school Timothy appeared to be struggling academically. His form teacher was almost apologetic when talking about his examination marks: 'It sound cruel to say it but he hasn't really got many strengths, apart from the fact that he gets his nose down and he tries. I mean look at his marks in all his subjects, apart from art where he got 50 per cent, but in science he got 8 per cent and in my social studies he got 9 per cent, in maths he got 16 per cent, which is a measurable one, I mean in maths you're either right or wrong, aren't you? Now language and literature, English, which is open to interpretation and generosity of marking, now even that he only got 29 and 30 per cent. Woodwork, I believe that must have been theory, he only got 5 per cent. He really is quite poor.'

It was clear that no teacher thought that his lack of success was the result of poor behaviour, as was the case with some of the children in the group. The comment made by his form teacher was typical: 'He's not disruptive at all. He sits and mutters to one particular lad. They talk, not disruptively, he gets on with his work. His writing's a bit slow and lazy, but he plods on and he's nearly always not finished when the rest have, but it's not because he's messing about like some of them. He's been labouring away and doing his best. As I say, he's no problem whatsoever discipline wise, and I must admit if we're not careful I think he can tend to get ignored because there are one or two kids who can be quite disruptive, attention-seeking. He's a blessed relief in the corner, you know? And it's probably not fair to him in a way, though I don't know the answer.'

As can be grasped from his examination results, Timothy was at the bottom of his group academically, which, in the case of maths, came as something of a surprise to his teacher. In commenting on his examination performance he said: 'His efforts were very poor. In fact they were so poor I didn't give them back to him. I just gave him an estimated mark. He virtually didn't score on one of the tests.' Yet in class he had thought that Timothy had understood the concepts.

Ironically maths and geography were Timothy's favourite subjects. Other subjects were less well liked either because of difficulties of teacher control or because of lack of interest in the way they were taught. For example, he disliked general science because the teacher was 'too soft' and allowed pupils to disrupt the lessons. 'People are getting up and throwing things across the room. She doesn't say nothing to them, she just sits there.' His poor opinion of social studies was for a different reason: 'Because all you do is talk. You could drop off to sleep when you're listening you know. I'd rather be writing than listening.'

When Timothy was asked about his academic difficulties he appeared to show little insight, concentrating almost exclusively on his writing difficulties. In particular he had problems doing what he called double writing, i.e. joined writing. He had always used printing at the special school. Reading joined writing appeared less of a problem for him but he found it difficult to copy such writing from the blackboard. 'It's not hard reading them, it's when I have to write them.... You just have to think about what it says. I pronounce it and see what it sounds like, and if I think it makes sense I write it down.' A factor that probably did little to help Timothy was his extreme reluctance to ask for help. If he could not do something he would simply leave it and continue with something he could manage. For example, when he had difficulty spelling a word he would not ask. 'I feel daft really. No one else goes up and asks I don't think.'

Jonathan assumed what his teacher described as a black and white approach to his work. If he thought he could do the work he would attempt it, but if he thought the work too difficult he would do some work from a file provided by his special needs teacher especially for such occasions. Although Jonathan had lessons with children in years other than his own this had not proved to be a problem, as his special needs teacher explained: 'They just seem to treat him as part of the form. He just seems to be able to adapt to wherever he is. If he's with the first year he adapts to them.... Where I couldn't fit him into an option, where either he couldn't do anything in that option column or there was nobody willing to take him, he's followed me, so sometimes he's been in with the first years and sometimes he's been with the fifth years and he's just joined in with the work a lot of the time.... He's just a great big, lovable lad and everybody likes him you see.'

Despite the affection that Jonathan appeared to generate he was, in academic terms, 'at the bottom of the pile'. However, his teacher pointed out that this did not affect his competence in other areas, such as social skills. In more specific terms his use of the four rules in maths work was at about the level of a 9-year-old. Language was also a problem in maths because, although he could often remember what he had read, he could not read very well. As such he found it extremely difficult to read the instructions. This difficulty also showed itself in housecraft, where he could not take down the recipes, and he scribbled to cover this up. In English his written work was very poor and he appeared unable to retain curriculum content. Nevertheless, his oral work, like Timothy's, was good and he was able to prepare and give a talk to the class with confidence.

Not surprisingly Jonathan liked best those subjects that required little writing, e.g. woodwork and PE. Nevertheless, he had no great dislike for any subject despite having particular difficulties in care, where he could not keep up with the work. 'There's too much writing. I'm a slow writer and I always do it for homework.' He said he generally found the work more difficult than he had at special school in that he had more to do and had to keep up with other children in the class. He said that when he was stuck on a problem he generally asked for help, but that sometimes he simply guessed, even when the answers were wrong.

In order to assist Jonathan's learning, and those who taught him, the special needs teacher had provided Jonathan with a file of work that she thought he would be able to do on his own. Thus when he was in lessons where the material was too difficult for him he could do work from his file. This idea turned out to be successful as far as the teacher was concerned.

Sarah and Peter

Sarah and Peter transferred from the same special school to different comprehensive schools at the age of 11.

Sarah was considered by her ordinary school teachers to be highly motivated to succeed academically. Sarah's teacher said: 'She is like the perfect pupil. She is nicely behaved, a charming girl and she certainly works with interest, whereas there are girls in this form who have such a poor attitude that they are immediately noticeable.'

Despite this glowing appraisal from her form teacher it was clear that Sarah's attitude was tinged with anxiety, affected by a fear of failing again in mainstream education. She had been worried in both a social and an academic sense about the fact that she came from the local special school. In a social sense she was afraid of being rejected by her peers. In an academic sense she was afraid of failing. Although she was described as being highly motivated and surpassing in academic performance those more able than herself, she reacted very badly to mistakes. Fortunately, her confidence had increased as the year had gone on. 'I think she is very conscious of the fact that she came from [special school]. I'm trying to remember whether she actually told me, or perhaps her mother.... I think her mother came in and told me that she really did feel very conscious of the fact that she came from [special school]. I think Sarah has mentioned it, but perhaps not in so many words. I've been very careful not to make that public knowledge and she, of course, doesn't say anything, so from that point of view she's generally accepted as a member of the class in that they're not aware of it at all. Now I have heard her say that she does have friends in the second year from [special school], so I don't know that the other girls are actually *unaware* of it. Perhaps she doesn't have any need to worry at all. I think in fact in a social sense Sarah worries in theory. I know from Sarah that she was very concerned about her academic work and coping in classes and being able to get the work done and so on, and I think that the fact that she's found that she has, and that she hasn't done any differently from anyone else in the exam boosted her confidence.'

Sarah had come very low in her group in the examinations, although her teacher doubted whether the results adequately reflected her abilities. 'She was sixteenth out of nineteen with 43 per cent, which I think is quite respectable, and I feel that it isn't necessarily a true estimate of her ability in that when she has time to work at her own pace she's quite bright, capable and produces work differently.'

Sarah's own expressed attitude had changed for the better after transfer. She was reluctant to admit to liking any subject at special school and particularly disliked science because of the teacher: 'He was horrible, shouting and hitting everyone.... I didn't like it 'cos he was cruel to some of them.' Her attitude to subjects was much more positive in the ordinary school, the only subject she actually disliked being maths, and again it was because of the teacher: 'I don't like the teacher that we have. Sometimes she has bad moods and she takes it out on the class. She says we're going to do something nice and then we do tables.'

Sarah did not express any particular difficulties with her work and appeared to have particular strengths in imaginative work such as drama and creative writing, areas where she was able to project herself into the character she played or wrote about. Her weakness in these areas was in expressing herself in complete sentences, a difficulty that showed up particularly in comprehension work.

Peter was described positively by his remedial teacher as being always willing to work, although he tended to be unprepared for lessons and occasionally broke the school's rule concerning uniform. 'Uniform, shoes, things like that. He'll come with trainers on instead of shoes and that's against the school rules. He does have a pair. He never has a ruler and some of his equipment and this is what you find in this sort of group. But he has his books and does his homework. We had a problem at the very beginning that he didn't do his homework. He wasn't taking it home, he was leaving it in his desk, he wasn't putting it in his homework diary. But now he does his homework and it's returned at the proper time.... I kept him behind at night once or twice and he had to do the work in his own time, so obviously he's realized it's better to do his work at home.'

Initially Peter had been very quiet, but as he had gained in confidence he had become quite talkative. The teacher stressed that he was not a 'behaviour problem': 'He's talkative, he likes a chat and I found he didn't work as well within a group of four as he does on his own. He'll concentrate better if he's on his own.... It's quite funny in a way because he was very quiet at first, *very* quiet, and he didn't offer very much.... But behaviour at the school, he's not been in trouble, there are no great difficulties.'

Peter, like Sarah, was in the bottom half of his group in academic terms, but was not considerably behind. His major weakness lay in his written work and his spelling. 'He likes to discuss things, he'll join in and he'll answer questions, but when it comes to having to write it down, that's a weakness.' The slow pace at which he worked was said to be a major weakness affecting all his written work. He wrote slowly and laboriously, forming every letter very carefully, so that his work tended to be 'quite tidy'. He was also described as being 'not very imaginative', but the teacher tended to avoid setting creative writing tasks: 'They don't do a lot of creative writing at this stage because they tend to get very frustrated.'

Peter was described as being fairly strong in all areas of maths except his tables, but his knowledge of these had improved. However, as in language the speed at which he worked proved to be a problem, particularly in test situations. 'His main problem is speed—the length of time it takes him to do them—which in class work is all right, but when it comes to the tests they do he doesn't do very well because he doesn't complete as many as he ought to. It's not really a realistic test for him, he could do with more time.' Despite these two difficulties, it was clear that Peter was not significantly behind the rest of the class in maths. 'In other things he's fine. He perseveres, he tries very hard and certainly keeps up with the others.'

Interestingly it was reading rather than writing which Peter reported as being the most difficult. He had, in the special school, disliked reading intensely. He hated it because he got stuck on words and it was difficult to understand. After transfer some change in attitude occurred. Indeed he listed reading, along with maths and history, as his favourite subjects. It seemed that the ordinary school was working hard and effectively to improve his standard. In addition to the paired reading scheme the school had embarked upon, and which Peter participated in, he read on a daily basis to a reading specialist, for about ten minutes before lunch. There were no subjects that Peter said he disliked.

Anna

Anna transferred to the local comprehensive school at the age of 11. Her teachers indicated that she was motivated and had positive attitudes but that these were associated with social and emotional difficulties. She was extremely egocentric in her behaviour and this permeated her attitudes. She worked diligently but tended to be motivated by extrinsic factors. She sought, for example, to be first to finish her work and first to join the queue to see the teacher. These influences were ultimately harmful to her progress. For example, she constantly sought attention in English lessons even when she was capable of completing the task herself, and it was her behaviour that was said to be her chief weakness, affecting all her academic work. 'Her weaknesses tend really to stem from her overall view of the world. She is just not very capable of logical thought, it's all very egocentric. That's basically her problem and her weakness is that she will not try to reason things out for herself. As soon as she comes to a bit that she can't do then it's out to the teacher, demanding attention. Now it doesn't take very long to get it out of her, so you know, "You find it, read this passage it's in there somewhere". She'll find it with very little problem, but her weaknesses stem from this lack of self-confidence or attention-seeking behaviour, whichever way you wish to interpret it.'

Anna was in a remedial group of twelve children who were taught by subject specialists without remedial training in all areas except English, where the teacher was an English specialist with remedial training. In English-based subjects, those that required reading and writing abilities, Anna's teacher placed her above average in the group. Her reading ability was good, she had a vocabulary and was articulate. Her writing and spelling were also more than adequate although her writing tended to suffer slightly from a general lack of co-ordination.

In maths Anna's special needs teacher said that as a result of poor teaching all that could be assessed from her work was her mechanical work. The teacher who had taken the group for maths had since left the school. Her special needs teacher explained: 'He just wasn't suited to teaching these particular children in those circumstances and none of them made any significant progress whatsoever. It's affected the whole class equally. I should think they've all suffered equally.'

Despite her above average performance for her group, her social and behavioural difficulties, together with some lack of co-ordination, militated against her transfer into a mainstream class in the school. Anna was positive about the subjects she was studying, except for two. She liked English, 'cos I hardly have much problems with it', and domestic science and needlework, which were 'fairly easy to do and nice'. She disliked music and geography. Music was difficult: 'It's hard for me to do. You have to try and guess what rhythms that he claps or guess which notes they are and stuff.' Geography was a problem mainly because of the teacher: 'I don't like geography. I don't like the woman who does it, most of it doesn't make sense.' Anna's parents provided interesting examples of geography homework, and their reactions to them, which are portrayed in the next chapter.

SOCIAL INTEGRATION

Jonathan and Timothy

Although Jonathan had considerable learning difficulties he had integrated well socially. Because he transferred after spending nearly seven years in special school, social difficulties might have been expected, but they did not occur. He had been involved in various out-of-school activities with children from the ordinary school he transferred to, and was an accepted member of the community. 'Special school had not', commented his remedial teacher, 'isolated Jonathan.' He was a member of the Boys' Brigade and at school fellow members had tended to take a protective stance, an example, perhaps, of co-existence breeding understanding, and understanding in-ducing a sense of responsibility. This was certainly the view of his special educational needs teacher. 'He's very well known in [his home town]. His mother made a very good decision in that she sent him to Boys' Brigade and Boys' Brigade is quite strong in this school and you've got everyone from first year to fifth year in Boys' Brigade. In that organization they protected him and he's also got known, and so if I walk across from say a first year lesson to a fourth year lesson with him there are kids saying, "Hi Jon!" all the time. Everybody seems to know him and the boys from Boys' Brigade have sort of passed it on to others that, you know, he's [okay].... And I think really and truly they've protected him 'cos they've said, "he goes to Boys' Brigade, he's a bit slow but he's all right", and that sort of thing. So it was a wise move and he's Lance Corporal, so he's done well and it was a good move, so that even though he was at special school he didn't break away from the community.'

Although it was noted that Jonathan tended to associate with second and third years rather than with his own age group, this was not perceived as being a problem or labelled negatively as exemplifying Jonathan's immaturity. It was simply accepted as being Jonathan's choice. He had friends in his own tutor group, but he enjoyed the activities of the second and third years more. From a social perspective his teacher thought he had benefited considerably from the transfer. One factor that seems to have contributed to Jonathan's integration was that he had relationships with children in his new school that he was able to re-establish or develop following transfer.

Despite the fact that Jonathan appeared to have integrated well socially, he admitted to having experienced 'quite a lot of teasing'. Sometimes he reported this to the special needs teacher who in turn sent the culprits to the head teacher, and sometimes he gave as good as he got. In what appeared to be a long-running episode with a fifth form pupil, 'who called me "high-tech [special school]" each time I go near him', he simply called the boy names in return.

Unfortunately Timothy's social integration was less positive. Initially it seemed that Timothy was going to be very quickly accepted and happy at ordinary school. In the first term there seemed to be no evidence of any difficulties. The assistant to the adviser for special education, who had recently been appointed to the post after being deputy head at the special school Timothy and Jonathan had attended, described Timothy as having 'the social confidence to mix well'. After visiting Timothy in his first term at ordinary school, he commented: 'I wasn't worried about Timothy. He's probably as bright as most of them in the class anyway, the only difference being that he has never done "subjects". I wasn't worried about him when I went in. No problems at all, he's quite happy.'

Serious problems that had not been anticipated by anyone, including his special school teacher, did arise. By his third term Timothy was clearly in difficulty. Both his English and maths teachers were aware that Timothy was being teased. His maths teacher was particularly concerned. He thought that Timothy had become isolated socially, pointing out that he now sat alone in his lesson. 'I always felt there was some hint of bullying from the boys and particularly a boy called George, little taunts of [special school]. He now sits by himself, right away from the boys, which is a bit unfortunate. He used to be very friendly with Martin and that seems to have gone by the board now.'

Describing the situation as being 'a bit dramatic', he was contemplating suggesting that Timothy spend his final year at the school in the year below his own, with whom Timothy seemed to be spending much of his time. 'I think he seems far more attached to the lowest set in the third year. When they go for lunch he tends to go with them. And it looks a good unit, he seems to fit in far better with that unit.' He pointed out that Timothy had also played truant but was uncertain whether this had been triggered off by the end-of-year exams or whether this could have been a result of social problems within the class. Whatever the cause it had been dealt with 'gently'. 'Normally if they play truant they go on report, the coals are heaped upon their heads, but I think with Timothy it was dealt with very gently indeed.'

His English teacher was also aware of Timothy's difficulties, but had positive comments to make about how Timothy had integrated socially: 'Socially the mix [in the group] is quite a good one. He started off working alone and then he gradually got around him a group of friends and seems quite adjusted in the classroom.... The thing was basically it was quite a cohesive group of children, I'd got them round to my way of thinking, so it was a well-structured and well-disciplined class and consequently it was easier for him to come in there.' However, he too had noted some bullying, which had led him to make a definite effort to integrate Timothy. 'I went out of my way at times to integrate him and I went out of my way to stop some bullying which was going on from one particular person. [I] just started getting vibes, to used an old-fashioned word. There was some banter that was going on. To give you an example, Timothy had a coat, a type of lumberjack coat and it became the butt of certain ribald comments from one boy. He [Timothy] was certainly sticking up for himself. He allowed it to carry on of course, he didn't get angry, actually I don't know whether that's part of his make-up, he didn't seem to get particularly angry, not what I saw anyway, he tended to become much quieter, he didn't complain about it.' Like his maths teacher, Timothy's English teacher was aware that Timothy's attendance at lessons had fallen: 'There has been more absence this last [summer] term. He was very good at the beginning. I'm not his form teacher, so I don't know the precise figures but his attendance in English classes has gone down.'

The supply teacher with pastoral responsibility for Timothy's form was aware of Timothy's numerous absences but had not had any feedback about this from the head of pastoral care, who had dealt with the matter. 'I've not had any feedback on that. I've wondered, you get various notes, like he's ill, he's a sore throat, all the usual, fairly trite excuses. He does send notes. He probably feels depressed, a bit miserable at times, he thinks, "I can't do the work, I don't want to go to school mam, I've got a sore throat". I don't think he's truanting. I think he genuinely, you could say psychosomatic even, but it's probably genuine enough, coupled with fairly easy-going attitudes on his parents' part. I've not met them though.' Timothy was a good attender at special school, but his attendance at the comprehensive had fallen to 50 per cent by his third term.

Timothy had not experienced teasing or bullying at special school and explained his experiences post-transfer partly in terms of novelty: 'You get called a bit at first. [They] just called me [a derivation of his surname]. Also people said, "you come from [special school]", but I just say, "yes, I'm not bothered", just admit it. Some people don't call me now and some people do.'

By his third term it was clear that the teasing had increased rather than subsided and he and two of his friends had, at one point, taken action. 'I wasn't going to say nothing at first. It was my friend, Martin, he said "if you don't tell on them, I'll tell on them 'cos if you don't tell on them they'll talk more". I don't want any bother sort of, you know? I don't want to get anyone in bother, I don't bother.... I went to the staffroom, Martin knocked and John told and I was off next day 'cos I weren't feeling too good and when I came back Mr X [head teacher] shouted me across and he said, "who's been bullying you?" I said, "no one sir", and he said, "there has", and I said, "they keep teasing me every now and again", and he said, "if you have any more aggro off them, come and let me know about it straight away".' Timothy was uncertain whether he would actually take such action. 'It depends how bad it is. It's no use going to him over every little thing like calling.'

Interestingly Timothy was not impressed with the idea of joining the year below him. 'It wouldn't be the same 'cos moving in a new class is same as moving in a new school. I'd rather stay where I am.'

Sarah and Peter

Sarah's teacher had some reservations about how Sarah had settled in. She thought she was tense, shy and not as comfortable in the classroom as she might be. 'I think she's settled into the school and is coping with lessons very well indeed. It's more difficult to tell in social terms, particularly with Sarah because I think she is quite shy and quite withdrawn. She has one particular friend with whom she established a relationship right at the beginning and she works in informal group situations, such as drama and sometimes in English, very well. She seems to be liked by the other girls and there doesn't seem to be any problems, but I do feel that sometimes she doesn't give as much as she might, she still seems a little shy—perhaps it's shyness that makes her defensive.... I find her much, much easier personally on a one to one.' However, the teacher thought Sarah had relaxed a little more as the year had gone on. 'I think she's more outspoken.... She will speak out now if there's something on her mind, and she can take a joke in that she can accept teasing in the general sense.' Her confidence had grown.

Peter's teacher felt that his integration had been extremely successful. She felt that although Peter had been quiet initially he had mixed in very well socially and had grown in confidence. One factor in Peter's favour was that he had not been out of mainstream very long and transferred back to the same school that all his old primary friends had transferred to. Thus some relationships were already forged.

Both Sarah and Peter, when interviewed, expressed the view that they felt they had fitted in well, and expressed no particular difficulties, except that Sarah, of course, commented on her terror of anyone finding out where she had come from. This defensiveness was waning a little by the end of the year.

Anna

Anna had experienced social difficulties in her special school, being described by her teacher there as 'an extremely egocentric child' who did not relate well to other children. This view was reiterated by her ordinary school remedial teacher. Anna tended to intrude on others' conversations, sought the teacher's attention and found friendships difficult to sustain. 'She doesn't get on very well with other children and they don't get on with her because they can't understand her problems. She doesn't understand the normal sort of childhood phases of humour and the fact that you can have friends and you can disagree with them and they can still be your friend.'

Problems with other children tended to occur out of the classroom rather than in it. In class she gave all her attention to work. Out of the classroom she explored social relationships. 'What causes Anna to have problems with other children is "dead time". It's what happens at break, what happens at lunchtime, what happens in-between lessons because normally speaking we don't have many problems in the classroom. The problems in the classroom are attention seeking and therefore a problem between teacher and pupil, they don't tend to be between pupil and pupil and so she's cocooned in her little world of "I do my work, go and see the teacher". Now occasionally she'll get cross if someone knocks her or something like that, but that's no different to any other child. She's got a peculiar view of this queuing business because she thinks she ought to be first all the time and will push in a queue in order to be first and gets very cross if anybody else does it.... I think the great bonus of the needlework club has been to actually take her out of that and she isn't with the other children to be bothering them. Now I don't think it makes them reject her and say, "oh well, she goes to needlework and we can't", I think it "saves her", if you like, from getting into further situations. We did try when she first came to encourage this in other areas as well. She went to an educational dance class one lunchtime, but for various reasons she didn't carry that on. But it's trying to find some way of minimizing this time without saying, "Well if I give her jobs to do every break or lunchtime, or we give her specialist treatment, it's not doing her any good and it won't do the others any good. There will be no interaction." What I'm trying to do is not only to get her to live with other people, but to get other people to live with her.'

Just as there were problems during 'dead time' within school, there were difficulties on the journeys to and from school that Anna's teacher had dealt with as best he could. Anna was the subject of much teasing: 'When she first came we had some very serious problems in travelling on the school bus. She would come in and say, "everybody's picking on me on the bus" and I would say, "what exactly do you mean?" "Well, they call me names and they push me, and they kick me and they won't let me get off." Now when you investigate, as near as you can find out—it isn't always easy to establish what does happen—this business of wanting to be first on, this business of "this is my seat, I sit here". On occasions other children have got upset because she's put her bag on a seat and wouldn't let somebody sit next to her. She overreacts grossly to anything she thinks is a criticism of her. She's a bit ... "paranoid" is too strong a word, but she's convinced that everybody is ganging up on her all the time and she doesn't understand gestures of friendship or even when people are joking, so whereas most children can brush off a remark she will get very uptight and of course as soon as you do that with people there are plenty who are just going to keep stirring the fire and it took us a long time.... I had to see goodness knows how many people who travel on the bus. I tried to explain to them, not blame them for the trouble, but try to explain to them what the problems were and that the only way we were going to get round this was to actually sort of ignore her. It took quite a long time to sort that out and it does flare up now and again as well. It's very similar to what flares up in school on the way to lessons. Some children have made a very good effort to be friendly, but she doesn't recognize that what they are doing is being friends and she doesn't have much of a sense of humour, so when someone makes a joke she thinks it's serious. She's very serious and very tense most of the time. It's very difficult to get her to relax, so I have smiling practice with her.... She seems to see the world against her as if she's to fight them all off.'

He took a philosophical, long-term view of Anna's difficulties. His opinion was that social integration was a two-way process and that Anna needed to learn that her behaviour was unacceptable, while her peers needed to understand and make allowances for her. However, he was aware that this was something that neither party found easy: 'It's a two-way process and you've got to remember that kids coming into a remedial form intellectually are not capable of the kind of reasoning that you need with them to accept that her behaviour is unusual and therefore you've got to be more tolerant than you would in other cases. Because most of them are people who are going to turn around, if their normal reaction is to turn around and slosh you, they'll just carry on without thinking.'

Despite the obvious problems, Anna's teacher did not think that her transfer to ordinary school had resulted in deterioration in her social behaviour, although neither did he think there had been a vast improvement: 'I don't think the problem has changed very much. I'm not convinced really that it's improved very much. I'm also not convinced that it would have altered anywhere else either. I'm not suggesting that we've necessarily failed. I don't think even if she'd stayed at [special school] that the problem would have been made any easier.... I honestly can't see any way out except a fundamental change in her personality.'

He thought one helpful aspect had been Anna's transfer into the first year. Had she stayed any longer at special school he thought she would have probably ended up not making the transfer at all. He considered a transfer at 11 to be the only hope for a child like Anna. Other children had made the transition at other ages, but the teacher felt this increased difficulties for the child and that it took a very resilient child to withstand the kind of treatment children sometimes meted out to newcomers when friendship groups were already formed. 'Had she stayed at [special school] she would have had to stay there through to the fifth year because I don't think there would be any chance of making the transfer at a later age and then trying to fit in. The advantage that she had of coming in September was that the other children just took her as one of them. When a boy in the third year came in [from a special school] they knew—"here is a new boy" and what his background was and he had a bit to put up with at first. But he's a very resilient personality who's had to put up with an awful lot during his life and this was chicken feed to him. He's a great extrovert and it got him accepted in very little time at all. But you see with Anna it's very, very different.'

Anna recognized that she had not managed to establish satisfactory social relationships. Towards the end of her first term she commented: 'I've got a few friends in different forms, but not in ours because they won't make friends. They've been mean to me a bit, calling me Buggy and things.... They say I've got bugs and I haven't, and they say, "you're thick as well as going to [the special school], thick people go there", and I say, "I'm not", and try and ignore them about it.'

She had a half-cousin at the school but even this relationship was already fraught with difficulty by the end of the first term. 'She doesn't really like me hanging around her and talking to her when she's with her friends. She sometimes shouts at me and tells me to go away, but she does like me, her friend said. She doesn't like me hanging around her all the time 'cos I did at first but now I've stopped.'

At the end of the first year the situation with her form peers had not changed: 'Most people in my form and that form [Anna points to a nearby room] keep picking on me and most of the first years do. I've only got one friend in the first year. They thump me and kick me and stuff like that and they pick on me on the bus.'

TEACHERS' VIEWS ON INTEGRATION

Thus far attention has been limited to teachers' perspectives on pupils and pupils' perspectives on themselves. But what of the teachers themselves? What were their thoughts on integration and their own role in that process? All felt that for a child with special educational needs to integrate successfully in a comprehensive school, certain conditions were necessary. Where some of these conditions were absent in their own schools there was a general unease about the demands that were being made on them and that might be made on them in the future. For these teachers the issue seemed to be one of whether already scarcely adequate, or inadequate, resources were capable of responding to what could prove to be a further demand. In cases where provision for children with special needs within the school was seen as being adequate the question of integration rested almost solely on the needs of the child. In such schools teachers seemed happy to entertain the idea of children with a degree of needs similar to those who had recently transferred to the school, but were uncertain about whether they would be able to cope with children with greater needs.

Timothy's English teacher was one of those who felt that provision within the school for children with special educational needs was not catering adequately for those already in the school, let alone those who might transfer to it. He thought that the six children from special schools who had been integrated into the school had highlighted flaws already existing within the school. 'I think the children who have come here from the special schools have highlighted to a number of us the flaws which have existed in our own organization. I'm not sure the authority have thought out their policy towards integration, they're having to do it I presume because of political pressure, parental pressure and economic pressure, in so far as special schools are expensive, but they haven't thought about it.... The special adviser spoke of having a policy of Scale 4 senior teachers in the authority to come down and help in schools. Now nothing has happened at that level. I assume it was just a suggestion which was floating round the education offices, but it's a pity they haven't done something like that. I don't think even Scale 4 senior teachers are necessary—you just want people with specialist skills to come and help in the classroom and then when you build up the relationships then they can start passing on their knowledge to teachers.'

Like many other teachers in the school, he thought that if the authority's policy was to integrate children with special needs then support should be provided for the ordinary schools in the form of extra staff. 'If the LEA devised a policy which meant that already busy teachers didn't have to do more, that resources were available to implement the policy and that there was back-up if the policy was going wrong—I would accept it.'

In contrast, in Sarah's school, where staff felt that children with special needs were well catered for, even though some review of the type of provision made was to take place, the issue of 'level of need' was paramount. The head of the remedial department thought that where a child's educational needs were not generally greater than those of her peers with special educational needs the child could be easily absorbed into the system. If the child's needs were greater then the issue of resources would have to be faced and dealt with. 'It depends how low down the educational ladder they were. If they were very low we would have to have more staff to cope with it, but as long as we get more girls like Sarah we can cope with the situation. The three we have are really better than some of the others. Their work is better and we have noticed that their reading levels are higher than some of those who come from the other schools.'

Jonathan's special needs teacher took a similar stance. Jonathan was an 'amiable lad' who had integrated well, but this, she was aware, did not mean that all such children would integrate as easily. The head teacher of the school said that he would not find integration 'unacceptable', provided he was given the resources to enable him to provide suitable courses for them. While he thought that good provision had been made for Jonathan, he thought it would be impossible to cater for a number of these children individually in the same way: 'It would depend on the provision. I wouldn't find it unacceptable, providing we were given the resources to be able to create the sort of courses that were needed. Now that doesn't fit in necessarily with Jonathan and so he can follow some classes and may or may not take some exams at the end of it, but for him to follow a kind of timetable, seven subjects, all of which are examination-based, doesn't make sense, so we've had to take him out of some of the options and he's had to have an individual programme which [his special needs teacher] has devised for him. Well, you can do that for one, maybe two of them, but if you give more than this clearly that system doesn't work and you've got to start devising something as a group activity, then you need more resources. You need more resources in terms of having staff to teach, because it's no good just saying, "oh, you can teach O-level French this period and teach this group of children with special needs this period". You've got to train them, you've got to have staff who know exactly what they're doing and why they're doing it, who know exactly what the aims are and the objectives are because basically all here, virtually everyone, thinks the aim is to take a public examination at the end.'

Likewise, Anna's special needs teacher was very much in favour of integration for 'ESN-M type children' but again felt resources to be the major stumbling block. In his opinion ordinary schools had much to learn from special schools in terms of the type of courses they provided for their children: 'Very much in favour of the ESN-M type child. I think we in the ordinary school have got a lot to learn from the kind of courses that are provided for them in special schools in the later years, particularly thinking of [the special school Anna transferred from] and the links with industry and vocational training. I rather think that we've had a lot of pupils through this school who'd have been better going there part-time in the fourth year and fifth year than sitting here through examination courses when they weren't going to enter for the exam, when they weren't capable of passing it and the content of the syllabus was of no relevance to them, so we have a lot to learn to try and get into our fourth and fifth year curriculum the broad life-skills approach the special schools were very good at.... If we can bring that into the ordinary school we can do a very good job from years one to three with people who are slow learners and I think the environment is such that their social development in most cases is going to be enhanced by being here rather than at [special school]. The opportunities they get for sport, contact with clubs and societies with other children I think is greatly enhanced.... But I think as a school we've got an awful lot to learn with what we do with the fourth and fifth years. So certainly I would be happy to see these children integrated here and in many ways it would be easier to deal with six or eight than it is to deal with the odd one.'

He recognized that the school, as it was currently resourced for children with special educational needs, posed a problem: 'The greatest difficulties, I'd put it down to three I think. One is that there isn't anybody else on the staff that is specifically trained or has had any of the kind of experience I've had with dealing with slow learners or children with special needs or anything else. That's a problem of resource. Secondly, I think that I've got too many responsibilities outside of special needs to be able to spend time within that area. Time is the most precious commodity. I've got a full teaching timetable, I've got the responsibilities of housemaster, which goes across the whole spectrum of ability, age and everything else, and an increasing responsibility within this area of special needs and I think something is going to have to go, but there we are. If I had less time in the classroom and more time to be as an individual within individuals it might help, but if another teacher was appointed as another remedial teacher to do some of the withdrawal work and so on, that might help. The resources of time are very important. The third thing, which is of overriding importance in secondary schools, is that no matter how clear you are on your philosophy the timetable and the physical organization of the school is absolutely paramount and that whatever you think would be a good idea, unless you can justify it in all sorts of ways, and usually the educational one is the last one on the list, it has to be able to fit in with the timetable, it has to be able to fit in with the staffing, facilities and so on.'

Peter's teacher was the only one who did not mention the issue of resources in relation to integration. Her comments focused singularly on the nature of the child's response to transfer: 'As long as they are confident and happy I think that integration works very well.'

When asked more specifically about their ability to cope with the transferred children four of the five main teachers said they felt able to cope, but their responses were qualified, affected primarily it seemed by the quantity and quality of the provision made for children with special needs in their particular schools. Where provision was seen as being inadequate in some way, teachers felt they had coped less well. Where provision was thought to be adequate, the focus was then placed by teachers firmly on the nature of the integrating child.

Anna's teacher was one of those unhappy with the provision currently made within his school. Although he thought he could cope in terms of his own professional expertise, he identified time as being a crucial factor and as being something that was not available. 'I feel quite honestly that I would be quite happy handling far more problems in terms of expertise. What we need is time and opportunity to get together and counsel these children. You see I see no way out of this particular problem except through continual counselling of Anna and other children, it's not just me to her all the time. I don't see her problem mainly as the academic problem, I think the social problem is such an overriding one that the other one pales into insignificance at the moment. I feel adequate for dealing with her on a personal level, what isn't adequate is the opportunity that I get to actually resolve a situation when it occurs. It's not possible to sort of down tools to find out what is going on. There is not that amount of time. There is not that amount of time to sit down in a tutorial period and discuss and develop these social skills, which would help the other children as well. I think these organizational problems are too vast.'

This teacher said that he would have preferred to have a number of children with the same type of difficulties rather than one. It was impossible to weave a teacher's timetable around the needs of a single child. 'In many ways you're better off having ten of these children and keeping them than having one and putting them in with a bunch of others whose problems are very different. Dealing with a one-off, whether it's an educational problem or a social problem like this, or I've had in the past a child for whom English was a second language on the grounds that "there aren't many children in there, so you will have more time", now it doesn't work and if you've got a one-off of anything you've got to carry on your normal work and do another thing in-between'.

He thought that Anna needed someone to be with her constantly and to intervene where necessary when Anna landed herself in social difficulties: 'What we could do with for Anna is somebody to actually be with her most of the time which would entail going with her to other lessons, sitting with her in other lessons, even if under the guise of helping the class generally, but being there to intervene at the point of crisis. What we can do is mop up afterwards, but intervening at the time is very difficult because these things tend to happen in unstructured time, at breaks, in lunchtimes and between lessons, so that's the kind of resource we need.' In-service training had contributed, but his own skills were unique in the school and he lacked the advantage of working within a supportive department.

Timothy's maths teacher also thought there was a gap between what circumstances demanded and what teachers felt capable of doing. The difficulties he experienced in dealing with Timothy were as much to do with the nature of the group Timothy was placed in, and the provision the maths department was currently making for that group, as with Timothy's nature and educational difficulties: 'The biggest problem has been behavioural, the people with problems in terms of behaviour, and talking to Timothy while there is something happening in the background. He can get ignored if you're not careful. That's the biggest snag—if the boy is quiet he could be ignored.' This is not to minimize the difficulties that this teacher would have found in handling Timothy's educational problems even if the additional problems presented by other children in the group did not exist. 'I feel I'm inadequate in this situation. Within class, yes, he does good work and the results seem all right, he gets his work right, but apart from that....' He saw in-service and additional resources as being measures that might remedy the situation.

The English teacher also lamented the absence of specialist help: 'As far as discipline is concerned there is absolutely no problem. I'm a strong teacher.... I've learnt a few tricks of the trade.... He needs specialist remedial provision which is not available in this school, to be quite honest. I think he's come into a stable and friendly environment socially. Educationally I think he's come into a school environment which hasn't got the specialist remedial facilities to cope with his needs, to be quite frank.'

Where provision was generally felt to be adequate the question simply became one of the nature and difficulties of the child who had integrated. For example, Sarah's teacher commented: 'I take the approach that I treat all children exactly like each other, as children who will respond to similar things, that if you are fair, if you are kind, a bit of humour.... Lessons don't need to be a drag and school doesn't have to be like Colditz. All children will respond in a positive way to a slight hand and I find that Sarah responds very positively with kindness and interest on my part. Certainly I don't feel that I have to "handle" or "deal with" or "cope" with Sarah in the way that one might. She's not a problem child at all. She is the sort of pupil one would like to have in a class.'

Jonathan's teacher also credited her ability to cope to his personality. She thought she was 'very lucky' with him as he had fitted in easily and was well adjusted. However, she doubted whether she would be able to cope with a child who had similar learning difficulties but was less amenable. She felt an in-service course 'geared to the ESN-M child' would be beneficial to her.

It seems noteworthy that three of the five teachers mentioned either their past training or the need for in-service training when asked for their views on their ability to cope with the transferred child. Such training was apparently valued. They felt either that it had helped them to cope or that it would enable them to cope better in the future. Timothy's English teacher saw the need for in-service training and the need for a satisfactorily resourced environment as being inseparable. 'I think the in-service for the whole of the remedial area in English is vital and under-stressed. In-service training is important. What the authority seems to forget is that it's no use if you don't then provide the environment into which the in-service training can fit and that's what they don't do.'

Finally, most of the teachers bemoaned the lack of outside assistance. In none of the cases had the psychological service monitored the transfer process or the progress of the children after transfer. Only Anna's teacher spoke positively of them, describing them as being good and willing to help with diagnosis. Nevertheless, he was quick to criticize her statement, which, he thought, should have provided explicit guidance on how her needs could have been catered for. It had consisted of only three sentences. 'It wasn't really helpful except in the sense that a legal document does exist and because it does the review procedure must take place.... The explanation [for its brevity] was that it had to be done very quickly while they were at [special school] so they rushed through and did the whole lot in June and July or whenever it was and did it very quickly without a great deal of investigation.... It should tell you what to do about this particular child's needs. Now if the authority are saying that "this child has special needs, but we think they can be catered adequately for in an ordinary school", I don't think that's any reason to say, "that's the end of the statement".' It had been a long time after Anna had entered the school that her teacher became aware of the existence of a statement. He did not see it until April, seven months after her arrival at the comprehensive, though he was not clear why it had not been in her files before this time.

SUMMARY

The quality of academic integration differed between those transferring at 11 and 14. The latter fared less well, both ending up at the bottom of the attainment pile. The difficulties in both cases were similar, Jonathan and Timothy having problems with such basic skills as reading and writing. Difficulties with reading meant that instructions could often not be read, which militated against successful task completion, and difficulties with writing meant that they could not progress at the same speed as their peers.

Those transferring at 11 made better academic progress and were able to keep up with their work. Nevertheless, both Sarah and Peter suffered from lack of skills in writing and, in Peter's case particularly, the slowness of his writing had predictable effects. Anna was perhaps the most academically able of the five children and was placed above average in her group. Her academic integration was spoiled only by her demanding behaviour.

Three of the five integrated reasonably well socially. Peter and Jonathan were the most successful, perhaps because they both had peer support. Jonathan was able to draw on the support of his colleagues in the Boys' Brigade, and Peter, who had not been in special school for long, was able to build on relationships previously developed in his primary school. Sarah's greatest difficulty in the early part of the year was her fear of peers finding out that she had attended special school. This fear of being stigmatized showed in her tenseness and shyness and slowness in building social relationships. Fortunately, it decreased as the school year went by and her self-confidence grew.

Timothy and Anna did not integrate well socially, but for very different reasons. There was every confidence on the part of staff that Timothy would have no such difficulties since he was socially adept and friendly in the special school environment. Unfortunately he suffered severe teasing and bullying to such an extent that the school seriously considered moving him down a year group. Timothy had a much more straightforward solution—he simply began to absent himself. Anna's difficulties were a consequence of her own behaviour, in particular her lack of ability to pick up social cues. Her behaviour was unacceptable to her peers and as a consequence she was either ignored, or teased and bullied.

Despite the fact that the quality of academic and social integration was mixed for these children it is worth noting as a postscript that all were clearly of the view that attending an ordinary school was preferable to attending a special school. On reflecting on their own attitudes and behaviour the teachers in the ordinary schools were in favour of integration and confident of their ability to cope with such children. There were important riders, however, particularly with regard to the provision of appropriate resources, be they staff, time or equipment. They also accepted that the integration of such children had messages for a reconsideration of school organizational policies. They bemoaned the lack of clear LEA policies, the lack of assistance from outside agencies and the lack of in-service courses to provide the enabling skills necessary for successful provision.

Chapter 6

The Integration Process.
IV: The Parents' Perspective

What of the third partner in the educational triad? Parents can, and do, play a powerful supportive role in the education of their children, and recent research on parental participation indicates that this role is most effective when parents perceive themselves to be involved in a collaborative endeavour. Was this the experience of the parents of the case study children? What were their thoughts on the education their children received in special and ordinary schools? What were their perceptions of their children's reactions to transfer?

In order to gain this kind of information interviews were held with parents after the children had spent eight months in their new school. They took place in the evenings, in their own home, and lasted between two and three hours. An interview schedule had been designed for this purpose and comprised five sections. The first concerned the child's placement in special school, and information from this was dealt with in Chapter 4. The second section addressed the child's educational experiences in the special school, and the third dealt with the transfer to comprehensive school. The fourth section dealt with the parents' perceptions of the education their children were receiving in their present schools, and the fifth was open-ended to allow any additional comments the parents wanted to make. Each interview was tape recorded and later transcribed.

Parental views on the education provided for their children in the special schools are considered first, to provide a comparison with that in the comprehensive schools.

EDUCATION IN THE SPECIAL SCHOOLS

The level of parental satisfaction with the children's education at special school was fairly low. All voiced at least some reservations about the appropriateness of the work set for their children, feeling that it was too easy. The most dissatisfied parent was Sarah's mother, who thought that her daughter had regressed rather than progressed at special school: 'At private school she was the neatest writer, doing real writing, was up to eight times table. They stopped that at [the special school], they went right back to square one, so the outcome was that she forgot how to do real writing. They stopped times tables, said they didn't do that at her age and said that if she did know it, she had learnt it parrot fashion, she hadn't really absorbed it. And my attitude was, "Well at least she knew it in a fashion", and I think when I was her age I probably learnt it parrot fashion.... It was learning of some kind which went out of the window when she went to special school.'

Sarah's use of counters in her maths work was seen as being yet another retrograde step and, dissatisfied with the school's practices, Sarah's mother took up the issue with the class teacher. However, she felt her action had been unproductive. She had always found the system defensive rather than open to the possibility that it might actually be at fault. For her there was no question of 'partnership'. She felt excluded and alienated. 'Do you know something? We've always felt that there's them and there's us, and although she's our child, you mustn't knock their way of doing things, and I feel that even now at [the comprehensive school]. You're not allowed to say what you think, but their opinion is the one that matters you see.'

Sarah had disliked the special school. She thought it was 'babyish', and referred to it as 'playschool'. However, though her mother saw Sarah's time there as having been wasted, she was unable to identify the kind of provision that might best have fulfilled her daughter's needs. This reflected a lack of awareness of possible alternatives, a lack of 'insider knowledge'. Sarah's mother and stepfather were simply unaware of the types of provision that were then commonly available for children with specific learning difficulties in other parts of the country. 'The only thing I can say is that I wish there was somewhere else that Sarah could have gone. I don't think the answer was leaving her at private school because she was very, very unhappy. She was getting bullied, picked on 'cos she wasn't able to do the work.' Sarah's stepfather commented: 'I think we didn't know enough about remedial classes in schools. I think although she started to slip and slip and slip in private school, I think she probably could have held her own in a remedial class. We weren't told about remedial classes and I think that the two and a half years at [special school] were a total waste of two and a half years of that child's life. It was a retrograde step, but that was the only alternative offered.... If we knew what we know now there's no way she'd have gone to [special school].'

Timothy's mother, who had herself attended the special school her son had attended, thought the ethos of the school had changed since she had been a pupil there. She thought discipline was lax and that too much time was spent in 'play'. 'When I went it was a damn good school and there was somebody, a teacher, always at the back of yer, over your shoulder, you know? And if you wasn't with your head down they'd go, "head down!", where now it seemed like a free for all—as long as they were playing games.' She felt there should have been a greater concentration on basic subjects, but had felt unable to criticize the school's approach directly: 'Things like that which weren't being done, but I mean you couldn't say nothing to 'em, could you really?'

Timothy's mother did not think that he had regressed at special school although she did think that the experience had not been particularly beneficial to him, especially during the last year when she felt that standards had deteriorated further: 'In a way he might as well have not gone to school, we might as well have kept him at home and let him do normal lessons here. He was just sitting there, playing games.' Timothy had complained of boredom at school and resented being given what he saw as simplistic work: 'He couldn't follow up why he didn't have no reading and things like that. He got more and more bored because, you know the ABC books? He had them, which was making him the mind of 4-year-old child really.... He used to throw them down the side of the couch and say, "I'm sick of them".'

Jonathan had been in the same class as Timothy at special school and, although his parents' attitude to the school was generally more positive than that of Timothy's parents there were some common criticisms. Jonathan's early years at the school had been a very positive experience for him, but the same could not be said of the final years he spent there, as the following conversation shows. Mother: 'The first three years, four years we were really pleased with him I think.' Father: 'The last one or two we were less happy with his progress.' Mother: 'We were happy with everything the teacher and the head teacher had done for him, but I felt Jonathan, at home, was beginning to want to do more and he used to say sometimes, "I'm bored, mum", and we didn't know how to cope with it. Sometimes he was bored at school and complained about some of the other kids being slow and messing about and "I can't concentrate".'

Like Jonathan's parents, Peter's mother had some positive things to say about her son's experience of special school. She thought it had 'brought him out and brought him on better'. But his case was remarkably similar to that of other children in one important respect—Peter had complained of boredom at special school. 'He used to come home and say, "Oh I'm bored, I'm bored, we do nothing all day hardly", but when I asked the teacher about it she said, "well we give them time, we don't push them on to this lesson and that lesson, we let them play a lot and do a lot of crayoning until they get confidence of everything that we do here".'

The parents who seemed to be most satisfied with the education provided for their child in the special school were Anna's. However, even in this case there had been difficulties and much dissatisfaction at the outset. Her mother said: 'On the whole we were very impressed. I think [the head teacher] is a very caring sort of person, he's not a PR man. I think as far as the children are concerned he cares for them very deeply and we had a lot of support from him. Unfortunately she made a bad start there. She started in September and almost immediately I sensed that she wasn't doing any work at all and I could feel it. She was coming home and saying that she'd sort of watched TV and done a lot of drawing and I sensed the frustration in her.... I knew without there being anything specific that she wasn't doing very much work. I felt, "she's only been down there a couple of weeks, there's no way I can go down to the school at this stage".' Anna's mother waited until half term, then went to the school. 'It's just not my nature to make a nuisance of myself really, but when you have a child like Anna you've got to stand up and fight for her because if you don't no one else will. I started very hesitantly to say that I didn't feel she was doing the amount of work I felt she should be doing and I was greeted with open arms—"at last we've got a parent who's complained! This teacher is absolutely useless, we've done everything to try and make her pull her weight and we can't".'

The result of this was that Anna was moved into a different class the following day and Anna's parents, at the head teacher's request, wrote to the chairman of the governors of the school to make a formal complaint about the teacher. Despite the possibility that this experience could have soured their view of special education, it did not. They saw the problem as lying with that particular teacher rather than the school, and the episode as simply being unfortunate. Anna's mother commented: 'That first term was so sad because at least she'd been used to a structured learning environment at [the ordinary primary school] and this woman was just marking time, just keeping them occupied, full-stop.' Possibly one factor that had helped Anna's parents was that they felt the teacher had not had too great a negative effect on Anna. Although Anna had not been working, she had not been upset. They did notice a change in her behaviour at home, which seemed worse during her first term at special school, but they were uncertain whether this was a result of change of school or boredom at school.

Thus, academically, all of these children had experienced difficulties, but the difficulty they generally faced was not of finding the work too difficult. On the contrary, finding the work too easy and too 'boring' was the major problem reported.

SOCIAL INTEGRATION IN THE SPECIAL SCHOOLS

The issue of how their children fared socially at special school was treated with as much seriousness and concern by the children's parents as were academic issues. All the children had experienced some kind of social difficulty, some within the special school, some outside, and, in some cases, in both environments. For example, although both Jonathan and Peter had faced few problems in school, out of school they were teased. Neither of them had found this easy to handle and, on occasions, had responded violently. Peter's mother commented: 'He used to get called for going to [special school] and that used to upset him a lot. He used to get it from friends in the neighbourhood—used to say he was a "nutter" and things like that. He used to cry with that, but kids are cruel really.... There used to be fights and that after school, but you know he's a tough little lad, he can handle himself.' Comments made by Jonathan's parents were similar. '[Jonathan] had a lot of problems with children in the area saying, "he goes to loony school". That upset him and a couple of kids got thumped.... I had to tell Jonathan to be careful because he's a bit of a strong child.'

Sarah had also been subjected to much teasing out of school and it had greatly upset her. She was acutely aware of, and embarrassed by, the stigma of attending special school and cringed and whispered her response when asked which school she attended. Neither was special school itself without its social problems for Sarah. She had friends, but these she tended to boss, a behaviour her mother found difficult to reconcile with Sarah's behaviour at home. 'For once in her life she was "top dog", like, you know, she'd got plenty of friends and she used to boss them about apparently. I got that impression off her form teacher.... I thought she was talking about somebody else's child.'

The teasing Timothy experienced out of school was also coupled with some difficulties in his relationships with certain of his special school peers. As with the others he was upset by the teasing he was subjected to out of school: 'He had a lot of that [i.e. teasing for attending special school] but it got to that pitch where he accepted it and used to say, "all right, I'm a loony, okay, you know now." But at the same time he must have bothered because he used to come in and tell us.'

Although he had friends at special school, and was not unpopular with his class-mates, Timothy's concern to do the right thing did cause difficulties for him at special school, just as it was to create many more problems for him when he transferred to the comprehensive school. His mother recalled one particular incident when Timothy had found some stolen bottles of whisky. He knew who had taken them and took the bottles along to his head teacher, revealing to him the names of the culprits. Not surprisingly this had not gone down well with those responsible for the theft. His mother said that in such instances Timothy thought he was 'being honest' and 'doing something good', but as a consequence life could be very unpleasant for him. He was called 'snitch' by certain peers and told he would be 'killed' after school.

Problems for Anna were greater within special school rather than outside it. They were generally the result of her very anti-social behaviour. At the primary school she had attended she had been in a class with children who had started school with her and were familiar with her behaviour. They had, explained Anna's mother, been 'a class of really good kids', who had 'been marvellous with her on the whole'. They had protected rather than rejected her. At special school her behaviour was less well tolerated. Her demands to be first in every queue caused particular problems. Her parents took a philosophical stance: 'She was shoved around and kicked around.... You have to accept this, when a child goes to a school like that, that there are kids from some very disadvantaged backgrounds.' However, although this show of aggression towards her behaviour did upset Anna, she was never reluctant to go to school. It seems that the characteristic that enabled her to behave in such an insensitive way to her peers in the first instance also enabled her to carry on in very difficult social circumstances.

THE CHILDREN'S FIRST DAY AT ORDINARY SCHOOL

The first day in the comprehensive school had passed much as might have been expected for three of the children. Jonathan, Peter and Anna's first days were not exceptional and were thus not discussed at length in the interview. This was not the case with Timothy and Sarah. Parents of both recalled their child's first day as having been particularly traumatic. The cause of Timothy's difficulties was the absence of anyone at the ordinary school to meet him and direct him to his new classroom and new teacher. Timothy's stepfather explained: 'We was of the understanding that he had to go to the head teacher's room, who would take him to where he was going, but the lad had to bloody find that out for himself didn't he? He went to [Timothy's sister who was a pupil at the same school]. It was like Timothy had been there two years. "Right, go to your classroom". He didn't know where the hell he was going.' Timothy's sister's form teacher had directed him to his classroom, but the saga did not end there because Timothy had got lost. 'By half past ten he said he wasn't even in a lesson. He said at one stage he was gonna come home, he were that fed up.'

Sarah also had a poor start, but this was as much a result of her anxiety to fit into the system and fear of not being able to meet the academic demands made on her resources, as of on any fault by the school. Her anxiety was extreme. Her initial excitement and happiness at being told she could go to ordinary school had changed shortly afterwards to feelings of apprehension, a state that had continued throughout the summer of the transfer and reached its peak during her first few weeks at the school. Her mother was very aware of her child's feelings and was very concerned about the first day. 'I dreaded her coming out. She's always been a bit of a loner ... didn't like it. "I don't think I'm going to fit in". That went on for weeks and weeks and weeks. In fact I think it was the fourth day she was actually cracking up, wasn't she? And I went down to the school because the headmistress had said, "if there's any problems get them sorted out before it gets into a great big issue". You tend to say, "oh, it's nerves, give her a week or two", but not with Sarah. You've got to do something straight away because she just gets herself into such a state. The main thing was, according to Sarah, "Do they know I've been to [special] school?—I can't do this and I can't do that—because they don't seem to and they're treating me as though I know everything." They never took the child on one side. They never acknowledged that they were in a remedial class, so Sarah got the idea they didn't know, that they'd put her in the wrong class'.

It seemed that on entry all the first year pupils had been placed in mixed ability classes and a week or so was taken to sort out where each child should be placed. Children were tested during this period, which exacerbated Sarah's anxiety. 'With Sarah not being able to read very well, these written tests that she was being given, she couldn't read them. This is what she was panicking about. "I can't even read it, let alone do it", and this is what I couldn't understand because I presumed that [Sarah's previous special school teacher] had gone down and shown them the work that Sarah was capable of. I must say I feel that she was thrown in at the deep end at first, and that was awful in my opinion because she needed careful handling as they all did in that class. It's a big thing for any child to go to another school and I think they should have been treated better.'

In her opinion, those in charge of the newcomers to the school should have been sufficiently experienced to be able to predict that this situation was likely to cause anxiety for those with learning difficulties and action should have been taken to avert it. 'They must be aware of this over the years, about the remedial class. They should have known better than to do what they've done. I mean your own common sense says, "Look, here's a bunch of little girls who've got learning difficulties who must be frightened to death. Let's get them together and explain what we're going to do." Maybe they did, but I got the impression that they didn't. That child came out terrified, really crying and not wanting to go to school. She was a nervous wreck.'

ACADEMIC PROGRESS IN THE ORDINARY SCHOOL

Most of the parents thought that their children had, in general, improved academically during the time they had spent at ordinary school. Sarah's stepfather commented: 'I'm sure she has come on a lot since she went to [comprehensive] school because in all honesty when she was at [special school] she could barely string a sentence together.' Her mother added: 'I mean, "the cat sat on the mat" sort of thing at eight and nine.'

Peter's mother, although not critical of the special school Peter had attended, was similarly happy with her child's progress: 'I think he's coming on smashing with his reading and there's some quite big words he's read himself.'

Jonathan's mother also talked about what she saw as being a great improvement not only in her son's academic attainments but also in his confidence. She gave the credit for this to Jonathan's special educational needs teacher in the school: 'She's worked wonders with him.'

The parents of Anna and Timothy were less than happy about their children's progress, because they believed that their children's abilities to handle the demands in the tasks provided were being seriously overestimated.

Anna found more than one subject difficult, but geography was a major bugbear, and the blame for this was laid firmly on the teacher by Anna's parents. Not only were the tasks she set for the children too difficult, but her approach to the children was seen as leaving much to be desired. 'I mean she may be a very good teacher for O and A levels. She calls Anna, the latest is "a little maggot". It used to be "a stupid idiot" or "a slag heap". Now this is a teacher in a supposedly caring, Christian school.'

Anna's parents had tried to play down this problem and as a result Anna was not reacting to it in an extreme way. However, it was clear that her parents felt strongly that such behaviour was unsuitable in a teacher, and were very aware of the power this teacher had to demotivate their daughter. 'Now fortunately Anna isn't worrying too much about this because we've tried to make light of it. [Another daughter] last year at her comprehensive school had a very strange English teacher who caused us no end of amusement or frustration or whatever. We sort of said to Anna, "You remember how we used to go on about her English teacher? ... There are always funny teachers in schools." And she'll say, "oh it's Wednesday today" and I'll say, "oh great, you have your favourite teacher today!" We've tried to make light of it and she seems to have accepted this woman.'

Although the issue of the teacher's approach clearly irked Anna's parents most of all, the work set added to their dissatisfaction. Anna's mother described events surrounding one particular piece of homework that had been set for their daughter: 'It was absolutely amazing. They had these sentences and they had to fill in the missing word and they had all these geographical terms. There were odd easy ones, "island" was one and perhaps "mountain" or something. But some of them, unless you were doing sort of O-level geography, you really wouldn't be expected to know. She'd just given out this sheet and she said to them, "If you don't bring this back I'll twist your heads round". Now you can imagine how we felt sitting at home looking at this sheet and knowing that no normal 11-year-old should have been given it, never mind a remedial 11-year-old, and knowing what this woman had said. We daren't send it back and say, "This is a load of rubbish", we felt that we had to complete it. And what annoyed us most of all was that one question was a word with seven letters beginning with F and it was something like "_____ is a land use apart from towns and villages". Now the obvious answer is "farming" and she'd said to them. "I'll give you that one, it's "function",' and we said to Anna, "that does not make sense", and she said, "I've got to put it, I've got to put it, she gave us that one". I said, "well it doesn't make sense to me Anna, why don't you put 'farming' as well?" No, she wouldn't, she was terrified. Now that is ticked in her book—"Function is a land use".'

Anna's parents were also concerned about the type of work set in religious studies lessons. It focused on the Old Testament in a way that they felt was too complicated for Anna to understand and involved a great deal of copying. On occasions the class had to learn the material for a test, and although Anna's parents disapproved of the quantity and nature of the material their child was being required to learn, they felt it would be wrong to deprive her of support on those grounds. Whatever the nature of the material they always supported her so that she could conform. 'You feel you've got to give her this support. You can't send her back not having learnt it. No matter how you feel about it, you've got to, she's got to get on with it.'

The unsuitability of the tasks set for Anna was not limited to subjects such as geography and religious studies. Mathematics was yet another. Her parents had been 'horrified' by one particular piece of homework she had been given and her mother had intended to take it into Anna's old special school to show them the kind of tasks set for low attainers in the ordinary sector, but had decided in the end that it would be best not to 'stir things up'. Her mother described Anna's experiences of maths in ordinary school: 'She hasn't had a good time with maths, she's had various teachers. The first teacher, she wasn't a bit happy about him'. Although this particular teacher had left, problems had not ended, and more recently her parents had written a letter to Anna's class teacher because they felt the work being given to her was not at her level. The situation had improved for a while, but the effects had not been long-lasting: 'Not long ago she came home with a sheet of simple fractions, which were impossible. She hadn't had the practice of simple fractions. If she had a page of simple fractions, say multiplication, then let's go on to divisions or let's go on to additions and do loads of practice at each stage, but she just came home with this sheet of mixed fractions. We've wondered how the others are getting on. I know she said that some of them had done fractions at their old school and they could do them all, even the hard ones. I mean I sat with her and we worked through them all together, but left on her own she couldn't do them.' Anna's father said of her work in maths: 'What little bits I've seen it does not seem to follow a pattern. They're not working as they should and building, they're starting somewhere up here and finding out they can't do things rather than starting down here and working up to the level. It's not well structured.'

Homework was generally felt to be a problem and Anna's mother usually sat with her while they did the work together. As a general comment she said: 'Anna isn't getting the right level of teaching and work generally.... I feel that in a lot of the lessons they're doing the same sort of thing across the board. I would say that the other first years are probably doing similar if not the same work as these children are having to cope with. I feel pretty sure that the biology she brought home recently, human reproduction and so on, all the first years will be doing that. I can't see anything very much, apart from the English, that is geared towards the remedial children'. English, taught by an English teacher with special training in working with children with special needs, was the one exception to this. 'English is super, it's right at her level, it's absolutely right. In fact she said to me not so long ago, "I wish we could just do English all the time". She's aware.'

Their feeling that much of the work given to Anna was not really geared to her needs led Anna's parents to philosophize about the type of department they felt would benefit their daughter. Her mother said she thought children with learning difficulties should be taught by specialist remedial teachers using the junior school approach rather than a subject-based one. Her father regarded unfavourably the use of mixed ability classes at secondary level, which is interesting in view of the fact that one of the claims frequently made in support of mixed ability teaching is that it particularly benefits low attainers. The difference is that this claim is often associated with self-image and self-esteem while for Anna's mother and father the issue rested on the appropriateness of the work set for their daughter. 'How can you expect that teacher to cope with children who are obviously university standard and children who are equally obviously Anna's standard? You can't. You can't spread yourself that thin. It's wrong to expect the teaching staff to spread themselves so thinly.'

For Timothy, who was placed in the fourth year of a comprehensive school, one particular teacher seemed to cause him unhappiness because of his failure to cope with the work, and because the teacher made an issue of it. It is not clear whether work set in other subjects was too difficult, but having difficulty was not necessarily seen as being a problem. The critical point for these children was whether the teacher knew they were having difficulties and whether the teacher made them feel foolish or exerted pressure without providing help. Where the task was too difficult, but the teacher did not insist on the task being completed, for example, the situation was deemed acceptable. Timothy's parents were aware that there was one particular teacher Timothy dreaded, because he found it very difficult to keep up in the lessons, and the teacher punished him for it. 'If [Timothy] was in now he'd tell you what lesson he takes him for. He doesn't like going to that lesson and he always says to us, doesn't he? "do I have to go to school tomorrow?", because he has this teacher. If he's doing whatever on the blackboard, which is pretty quick and some of it he's doing in handwriting which Timothy can't follow ... he's just started doing handwriting, but because [the teacher] has done about eight lines and he's practically finished what he's doing on the blackboard, Timothy is just on the top line.' Timothy's peers, obviously aware of his slowness in writing and the teacher's reaction if Timothy did not finish his work, made the situation worse by deliberately distracting him. 'He's got somebody at the back of him sticking lead pencils in his back and they're chalking all over his blazer.' According to his parents, the end result for Timothy was that he was regularly kept in by the teacher, presumably for failing to complete his work.

Jonathan also experienced some academic problems, but it seemed he was subjected to far less bullying than Timothy and was in a far better position to cope with them. Pace and understanding were particular problems for Jonathan in care. The subject seemed to involve a lot of writing. During lessons he was required to copy from the blackboard and for homework the class was given printed sheets from which they were required to copy questions and answer them. The difficulty, Jonathan's father explained, was that Jonathan was still not writing very well and, like Timothy, was still printing. Although they thought his handwriting had improved since the transfer, they were aware that this was still a problem for him. However, he also had difficulty in understanding this subject. The work tended to focus on problems in relationships such as marriage. It was clearly a subject designed to deal with the type of difficulties the fourth years would have to contend with as adults, but Jonathan seemed to be out of his depth. 'He doesn't know how to answer the questions because he's never experienced it and we can't ... we can explain certain things to him, but not the finer points.'

His parents suspected that the maths Jonathan had with the specialist maths teacher had also been too difficult for him, but the precise nature of this problem had been difficult for them to determine. Jonathan did not seem to understand the work set for him for homework, but neither did he seem to care about getting things wrong. His mother explained: 'He kept saying to me different little things about his maths homework, like, "oh, it doesn't matter if I get them all wrong." So I said, "Jonathan, it does really. It doesn't matter if you don't get them all right, you're allowed to get some wrong, but it's not right to get them all wrong". I couldn't understand what he was trying to say and I thought, "maybe he's having a problem in school, maybe it's another child saying something different to him". I couldn't fathom anything out.' Rather than let the situation deteriorate further, his mother contacted the school and informed the special education needs teacher of Jonathan's rather worrying attitude. The teacher had said she would talk to the maths teacher and enquire how Jonathan was getting on. If she discovered there were problems she said she would get in touch with Jonathan's parents. As she did not do this Jonathan's mother presumed everything was all right.

Not all the problems that occurred in the classroom were of an academic nature. Jonathan's mother described one incident, which showed how academic weaknesses affected a child's ability to fit into the general structure of a school. In this instance Jonathan was unable to comply with a punishment set for misbehaviour because it was beyond his capabilities. 'One day he'd been mucking about with another lad in the corridor. The teacher catches them—they were only giggling and that, messing around—this teacher calls them and gives them a good shouting at and gives them lines each. But Jonathan has never heard of proverbs and he gave them a line or two to write as lines from this proverb. Well, Jonathan couldn't remember it you see and it bothered him. Now I didn't know. He came home from school quite delighted that he'd got lines. I thought, "well that's a change, at least he feels like one of the kids by getting these". I don't expect anything other than the extra help he gets with his English and his maths and that, I don't expect any other things, he should get told off with the other children. So he came home delighted that he'd got these lines. He said, "the only trouble is mother, I can't remember what I've got to write". So I said, "well, never mind, go to school on Monday, apologize to the teacher, but say you will do them, but you've forgotten". But he was petrified. Well, I can't blame him really, to be honest with you. Well he said on Monday he wasn't feeling well. I never gave it a thought, I'd forgotten about these lines over the weekend. He said he wasn't well. He said he felt sick and his tummy was upset and I thought, well, you know yourself if you've got the runs, I didn't know he didn't have the runs, but I thought, "well maybe he's been up in the night and what have you". So I said, "well, it's all right, stay off school for the day". Then the penny dropped. So I rang [Jonathan's special educational needs teacher]. I said, "look, could you just sort a little problem out?" She was very nice. He went into school Wednesday morning. He was happy to go in Wednesday morning so I knew it was that. Little things like that get Jonathan down.'

SOCIAL DEVELOPMENT

It was suggested earlier that parents were as concerned with their children's social and behavioural development as with their academic progress. The following sections consider parental views on the children's social experiences following transfer, and their attitudes to school.

Four of the five children were said by their parents to have experienced at least a degree of anxiety about how they would get along with their peers at ordinary school before they transferred. The child who seems to have been the most anxious during this period was Sarah. Her mother described her daughter's fears: 'She said, "Will they have to know I'm from [the special school]? Will the other girls in the class have to know?" That was the main thing. "I don't want them to know. What if I don't fit in? What if I can't cope with the work?" Basically she was just frightened to death she didn't fit in.' Although Sarah did not settle down at ordinary school in the first instance, as she grew to accept the environment by learning that rejection by the system and her ordinary school peers did not happen immediately and, moreover, that it did not seem to be imminent, her anxiety declined.

For other children, pre-transfer worries had materialized in disconcerting ways. Jonathan's parents received reports on how he was integrating socially from Jonathan's sister, who was a pupil at the same school. She had told them that one or two children had tormented him, particularly when he had first transferred, but that since then the situation had improved. His mother said: 'Most of the lads there and girls seem to either leave him alone, or just say a few words to him and that's it.' However, there had been occasional incidents that made it clear that Jonathan's presence was not passing entirely unnoticed. On one occasion a fourth year boy had rubbed a blackboard duster over Jonathan's jacket, and on another his jacket had been marked with black felt pen. On the other hand, if Jonathan was experiencing some problems at school, it seemed that teasing from children in the neighbourhood had ceased completely since his transfer to ordinary school. His mother speculated on why this was the case: 'Now whether they've seen him in his school uniform and realized that he can't be as thick as they thought he was I don't know.' His father added: 'Plus the fact he's grown up and filled out and he'll plant them one.'

One of Anna's main problems was in relating to people. It was not therefore surprising to find that she was experiencing some difficulties in this area at ordinary school, just as she had at special school. Her insistence on having her own seat on the school bus singled her out for teasing. Her bag tended to be kicked up and down the bus or children stuck their legs out so that she couldn't get off the bus when it came to her stop. Her parents again saw this as inevitable given the nature of Anna's difficulties. 'Kids know, as soon as you've got a kid with a behavioural problem, other kids know and they play on it.'

All these children seemed to cope with their respective problems, using strategies that were less negative in their ultimate effects than that used by Timothy. It may have made them very upset and anxious but they were all prepared to carry on dealing with their circumstances. The difficulty in Timothy's case was that he coped with the problems he was facing by withdrawing from the situation. Whereas he had been a lively and outgoing character at special school, at ordinary school he reverted to the withdrawn behaviour he had first displayed in infant school, which had contributed to the decision to withdraw him from mainstream schooling in the first instance. Along with general teasing, such as being called 'loony', there were more serious difficulties. His stepfather said that Timothy's uniform had been spat on, drawn on and had chewing gum stuck on it. He explained that Timothy's trousers were made fun of and that on one occasion they had been slit down the side with a pen-knife. In another incident when boys in Timothy's year were attaching electrodes to their ears, Timothy, instead of ignoring the situation as other children might have done, had told the head teacher. As a result he was called such names as 'squealer', 'teabag' and 'snitch'. When some pencils were stolen Timothy found some of the pencils in his pocket and took them to the teacher. It seemed that the culprits were trying to put the blame on him. In yet another incident, boys in Timothy's form had stamped on his fingers with the result that when he returned home from school his parents were so worried that they took him to hospital. They seemed to think that Timothy's problems were created by three particular boys in his form, but were concerned about reporting incidents to the school for fear of making matters worse. On only one occasion had his mother written a letter to the school, but this had had only a temporary effect. Things had 'quietened down for two weeks and then started up again'.

ATTITUDES TO SCHOOL

Two of the children were described as being very happy in their new environment. Jonathan revelled in the status of attending ordinary school, as his mother explained:

'He's pleased he's got a load of books he can carry around in a bag on his back, he's delighted with that. He doesn't use half the books … in the course of a week, and he doesn't have to take them every day, but he does.' Not only did Jonathan enjoy carrying books around, he also liked changing classes and wearing the school uniform, one of the things ordinary school children generally find distasteful. It is interesting that the things Jonathan relished about his ordinary school were things not found in special school. Jonathan's father summed this up when he commented: 'I think he feels he's one of the lads now.'

Anna was equally delighted but her pleasure came as much from her newly found sense of independence as from attending an ordinary school. Following a number of occasions when she returned from school upset because someone had been teasing her on the school bus, Anna's mother had asked her if she would rather go back to special school. Her response had been an emphatic 'oh, no way!' The other rewards were also high. In attending an ordinary school she had distinguished herself from her sisters. Her mother explained Anna's liking for things that made her different: 'She's always wanted to be different. Like I said, at play school she would never mix with her peers, she had to be with the staff…. Everything she's done she has to be different and the more different she is the happier she is, so going away on a school bus, even going to [special school], even though she was aware that there were children there with more problems and so on, she was thrilled because it was different from what children do. So [the ordinary school] is great, but the drawback is coloured by what's gone wrong on the school bus on the way home.'

The other three children who transferred had less positive attitudes towards school. Peter's mother said her son's attitude was generally good and that she never had any problems getting him to go to school. However, she did think than he had 'gone off' the particular school he was attending and wished he had gone to another, the one his brother attended, which his mother had initially wanted him to attend. The difficulty had been that the school had not been looked upon favourably by Peter's special school teacher who had arranged the transfer. She had been concerned that the school his brother attended would be unable to give Peter the level of special support she felt he required.

Sarah's mother thought that Sarah simply did not like school generally and that she was unlikely ever to like it. Her attitude to this particular school was no different. Even so, she did think that Sarah had settled. Although she had clearly found the actual transfer to ordinary school traumatic, she was now happier than she had ever been at any other school and had made friends. Her parents' view was that she was 'as happy as she'll ever be at school'.

Only Timothy seemed to much less happy than he had been at special school. His stepfather explained: 'I think he's far less happy there than what he was before. He's far from being comfortable … well actually it's that bad that if we weren't saying, "You've got to get ready and go", he wouldn't go. We think, "is he at school or is he not?".' Timothy had thought ordinary school was 'okay' only for the first few days. The beginning of social problems for him marked the end of that feeling.

The problems for Timothy were acute. His parents talked about him being tense on Sunday evenings and Monday mornings before the time came for him to set off for school. His mother said: 'He once turned round and said, "I feel like killing myself", and I said, "oh, Timothy, you're talking rubbish!", and he said, "well mum, if you had to put up with what I do". I said, "I'd just tell them what to do Timothy", and I thought, "well, I wonder if he really does mean it?", whether he's taking too much pressure and can't cope with it because he's nobody to talk to or anything.'

CONTACT BETWEEN PARENTS AND SCHOOL

Levels of contact between parents and schools varied considerably. While variation occurred in standard practice, teacher industrial action was a strong intervening factor which exacerbated these variations. Some parents had received written reports, but had had no personal contact with the school, while in other cases the reverse was true. In every instance there had been some communication between the school and the child's parents. The difficulty was that this did not always take a two-way form. This was the problem in Timothy's case, where the need for parent–teacher interaction was imperative. The school did send a report on his progress at the end of the academic year, but this was as far as communication went. Timothy's parents were not presented with a formal opportunity to express their concern about his happiness, although it is apparent that even if they had had this opportunity they might not have taken it. This was the clearest instance where two-way communication was badly needed and could have resulted in an improved situation for the child. In all the other instances, although communication initiated by the school itself was not always satisfactory and was, in some cases, non-existent, the need for it was less acute. Where there was a need the initiative was taken by the child's parents.

Sarah's mother, for example, had been concerned about two issues during Sarah's first year at secondary school. The first was Sarah's anxiety at the time of transfer and her mother, responding to the school's directive to get problems sorted out as soon after they were identified as possible, visited the school to discuss the problem with the head teacher. The second concerned the school's approach to sex education, which Sarah's mother felt had been unnecessarily abrupt, unnessarily crude and in any case premature. Thus, although she had not received a formal, written report on Sarah's progress, she had made five or six visits during the course of the year.

Sarah's parents were horrified at the way sex education had been approached. Her mother explained: 'The worst thing that I feel that [the ordinary school] has done to Sarah is the way they've brought sex education into her life, the way they've done it, I'm absolutely horrified. I had no idea they were going to do sex education in the way they've done it.' They had received no notification that their daughter was to be given sex education and it seems that lessons had begun five weeks into the first term. Sarah had been very upset by what she had been told, despite the fact that her mother thought that she was quite mature for her age and that if anyone in the class was to cope with it she would have. It was clear that she had not been ready for the experience. 'She was so upset and disgusted that she didn't want to know about men, marriage, sex, babies. She'd been really interested before. "How could you and daddy do such a thing?". You know? I mean we've all gone through this, but I couldn't have coped with it at 12 years old and the point is she didn't want to know, she wasn't ready, and if Sarah wasn't ready I don't know what the other children are like in that class, but she, to my mind is one of the more mature ones'.

Her mother had gone into the school to ask to see the books the class had been given, since Sarah had clearly perceived them to be pornographic. The head of year had not actually seen the books the particular teacher had used and would not let Sarah's mother see them, leaving her both suspicious and resentful. 'It's fit for my child to see, but I'm not allowed to see it. Now there's something wrong there.' Despite her strength of feeling Sarah's mother had refrained from taking the issue further for fear of some backlash on Sarah, and she was under pressure from Sarah to drop the issue. 'She doesn't want me to make any fuss about it because she thinks she's going to be picked on and all the rest of it, so her mum isn't allowed to say anything else about it.... We've kept our mouth shut for her sake. If she was at any other school and we hadn't had such a performance to get her back into normal society, I'll tell you what I would have done, I'd have gone through the right channels, found out what I could do about it and made a great big thing about it. We're keeping quiet because the system always wins and to make it a bit better for Sarah. But you see they've got you haven't they? You make a big performance and the child suffers.'

Sarah's mother felt that this experience had contributed significantly to Sarah's behaviour, the nature of which had changed over time: 'It's gone from Sarah being absolutely disgusted and upset about it to making cheap jokes about it now. I think it's the parents' role to tell the child, they'd had my child a few weeks at this point. How do they know how my child's going to react to that sort of thing? For a total stranger to tell my child the most intimate things about her life. It should come from me and I'll be the one to choose [the time]. That's what hurts me more than anything, that it's too late for her, they've done it and I cannot undo the damage they have done.'

Sex education was raised spontaneously by two other parents, although in these instances no attempt was made to contact the school. Anna's parents felt that it had been broached too early for Anna to understand it. She had not, they claimed, 'a clue what was going on'. Timothy, like Sarah, disliked the subject and appeared to be disturbed by it. His mother recounted that: 'He's told us recently he's watched these films about having babies. All this is new to him, it's not gone down very well like. He doesn't [like it], not one little bit.' This exposure to sex education was linked by Timothy's mother to some of the social problems Timothy was experiencing, perhaps because Timothy had shown an obvious dislike for the films that he had possibly been shocked by. For other children in the school the films may have been part of a gradual sequence, i.e. a planned course. Timothy seems to have been thrown in at the deep end and not reacted awfully well to the experience. 'He said that they call him queer, they keep saying he's a bumboy.'

Anna's parents, although concerned about how she would cope in the comprehensive school, experienced very little contact with the school. They had made contact initially by telephoning Anna's class teacher at the end of her first half-term, simply to ensure that everything was running smoothly. From the school they received a grade card at the end of each half-term, which gave them some indication of whether Anna was coping with her work, but they had not received a full report at the time of interview and the open evening planned for March had been cancelled as a result of teacher action. Like the mothers of Peter and Sarah, Anna's parents had met only a small proportion of the teachers who worked with their daughter, in this case only Anna's class teacher and the deputy head teacher.

Jonathan's case was the exception to this general trend of minimal contact. His parents were the only ones to attend a parents' evening during the first year of transfer, and the only ones to receive two written reports during that year, which covered Jonathan's subject areas.

PARENTS' VIEWS ON TRANSFER IN RETROSPECT

Views on the transfer covered a broad spectrum of opinion, ranging from Jonathan's parents, who wished their son had transferred to ordinary school sooner, to Timothy's parents, who wished their son had not transferred at all. Jonathan's parents were very happy with the support he was receiving at ordinary school. His mother commented: 'To be honest, I get the impression they've bent over backwards to help him.' Although aware that it was difficult to know whether Jonathan would have coped with ordinary school before the time came when he actually did transfer, they felt they would have liked him to 'have had a go' sooner than he had actually done so. They did not think he could have coped with transfer at the age of 11 but did think he might have coped at 13. They had thought about it at the time, but had not taken action becuase of their basic uncertainty as to whether it was the right thing for him, and because they were unclear about how they might instigate the process. No one had ever suggested to them that Jonathan might re-integrate: 'He's adapted to [ordinary school] quite well now, but if he would have started twelve months previous he might have been able to make a go of it, so I don't really know. But we feel that if he could have had a try at the third year it might have been all right for him, but there again we couldn't really do anything about it then because we didn't know how to go about it.... We didn't know whether it was the right or wrong thing.'

By the end of the following year Jonathan's parents were convinced that transfer to ordinary school was the right thing for him. Even if the special school had not closed down and provided a convenient time for transfer, they said they would have asked about the possibility of Jonathan transferring.

Despite strongly disagreeing with the school's approach to sex education, Sarah's mother did think that she was appropriately placed in the ordinary sector. Peter's mother thought likewise, but had doubts about whether the comprehensive school Peter had transferred to was the right one for him. Although she was satisfied with the education he was receiving and thought he was doing well, Peter had recently told her that he wished he had gone to the same comprehensive school as his brother.

Anna's parents had given some thought to this issue before the interview as they had been asked to contribute to Anna's statement. They were disappointed with the way in which the school had catered for her during her first year. They thought that only her special educational needs teacher had responded in a way that was appropriate and helpful. 'I would say that [the special educational needs teacher] was superb. He's a wonderful bloke, he really cares very deeply about the children, but I don't think he has the support from the other staff. My feeling is that he's working on his own for those children and that he doesn't have the support from the others. The others are not capable I don't think of coming down to the right level educationally. Some of the work is absolutely crackers, we've been so cross about it and once or twice we've felt like sending it back and saying "this is rubbish"—geography in particular, absolutely meaningless.'

There was a considerable discrepancy between their expectations of the nature and quality of provision the school made for children with special educational needs and the reality, as the following conversation shows. Anna's mother: 'Yes, disappointed, yes. We did feel it was going to be an extension of junior school. I think without [the special educational needs teacher] we would be very disappointed.' Father: 'It doesn't feel as we expected it to feel, does it?' Mother: 'No, definitely not.' Father: 'So we're disappointed in general terms—so far as her settling at the school's concerned, fine. How much of this is [special educational needs teacher] and his influence on a day-to-day basis and because she's in his class, we don't know. This is why we're anxious about next year of course, because she's going to lose him, she's going to lose that little anchor of that very, very caring person that she has been going to on a day-to-day basis. We just don't know how the next year is going to develop, how much of his influence has allowed her to settle as she has settled, even though she is out of her depth.'

They did not think they wanted to see Anna returned to special school. 'We don't feel now, in view of what we see now, we don't feel they have anything to offer her. In other words, although we don't feel she's getting what she should have at [the ordinary school], we don't see anywhere else where she's going to get what she should have. There's nowhere else we know of. [The ordinary school] was the nearest approach and we're disappointed from that point of view.... It don't have a remedial stream that we hoped for. It has not come up to standards that we hoped for. It is very sad, but it's something she'll have to cope with, that's all there is to it. She'll have as much backing at home as we can give her.'

Only Timothy's parents regretted the transfer having taken place. His mother said: 'I'm fully convinced I should never have had him moved.' However, with the move having been made, and given that Timothy was now approaching his final year and that this would be short, ending in May, she did not think it was worth transferring him back—a point on which she and Timothy's stepfather disagreed.

Chapter 7

Conclusion

POLICY

Since the publication of the Warnock Report (1978) there has been a central policy thrust for the integration of children with special needs into ordinary schools. The philosophical basis of integration has been well elaborated (e.g. Cope and Anderson, 1977; Kirk and Gallagher, 1979; Blankenship and Lilly, 1981); successful practice has been reported in Britain and abroad (e.g. Galloway and Goodwin, 1979; Madden and Slavin, 1983); and a 'common commitment to an integration principle' (Booth and Potts, 1983) has been reflected in significant texts on the issue (e.g. Hegarty *et al.*, 1981; Swann, 1981). The Advisory Centre for Education was thus able to state categorically that 'the integration of the handicapped into ordinary schools is accepted as an obvious goal' (ACE, 1981).

Despite this level of commitment there has been continuing disappointment at the degree of caution being exercised by LEAs in this regard (Thomas, 1985; Swann, 1985). Similar sentiments were apparent in the Select Committee report on the implementation of the 1981 Act (Education, Science and Arts Committee, 1987), an Act which required that children with special needs should, subject to certain conditions, be educated in ordinary rather than special schools. The final recommendation of the report read:

> It seems clear to us that a successful implementation of the 1981 Act is very much dependent on the development by an LEA of a clear and coherent policy, arrived at in a way which enables it to command the support of those ... who are most affected by it.

Their evidence suggested that there was a wide variety of LEA approaches to the issue of integration. Indeed the submission from HMI claimed that few LEAs had an overall policy at all.

This pattern clearly reflects that found in the seventeen LEAs studied, a pattern woven from several strands. There were clearly different philosophies operating on the role of special schools, but those philosophies were mediated by provision and demand, i.e. LEAs had very different populations of school types and pupil needs. HMI, in their paper to the Select Committee (HMI, 1987), commented on the substantial variations across LEAs in the identification of pupils to be statemented and this, in part, also seems related to the same factors. Thus, a child in an LEA enjoying lavish special school provision is much more likely to attend special school than an identical child in an LEA with little such provision. A final reason for lack of coherent LEA policies is the lack of resources, and in this situation the lack of a policy has distinct advantages. If there is no policy then no resources need be allocated. A combination of these factors—philosophy, provision, demand and resources—has thus led to the lack of an overt policy, underpinned by a covert policy of 'integration where possible'.

There are constraints on this covert policy. In addition to the inevitable consideration of resources at the levels of LEA and school, the major constraining elements were identified as negative teacher attitudes, inappropriate organization and curriculum, particularly in secondary schools, and inadequate teacher skills. Despite their acknowledgement of the importance of integration as an issue, it was not the issue that psychologists and advisers found most pressing—most pressing was making statements and their accompanying procedures.

The general picture to emerge from this study is that the potential for statements of special education need was great but that this potential could not be realized because of resource constraints. Particularly worrying to those involved was the confounding of children's interests with financial interests. This point is also stressed by Tomlinson (1988), who argues that 'an Act which encourages local authorities to meet the needs of pupils with learning difficulties in mainstream schools, without defining the provision required or handing over resources for this provision was, clearly, designed to upset a good many people'.

The Act theoretically opened the way to the creation of equal educational opportunities for children with special educational needs, but many LEAs had decided not to travel down that path. In all the authorities studied it was much more difficult to get a child statemented in an ordinary school, simply because of the resource implications. The outcome of this kind of policy was inevitable: either provision was in the form of a special school or unit or there was no extra provision at all. All too often, therefore, a statement was synonymous with special school provision.

The Select Committee noted the difficulties of resources. Not surprisingly perhaps, given that the Act enjoyed no specific allocation of extra government funds, the question of resources was the matter raised most consistently by those submitting evidence to the Committee. Two aspects were identified: a general shortage of resources in schools, and a lack of specific resources to implement the requirements of the Act. Both had militated against proper general provision being made. The Committee was 'in little doubt that a lack of resources has severely hampered the successful implementation of the 1981 Act', particularly the resources needed to fund the LEA's administrative costs of making the assessment and statements and of arranging properly funded placements in ordinary schools. It concluded that a 'commitment of extra resources is needed if significant further progress is to be made'.

The procedures for statementing came under heavy fire. The Committee argued that they take too long; parents find the language used and the complexity of the procedures difficult to understand; statements of need are vague and/or tailored to fit existing provision; and professionals contributing to assessment from different services do not respond quickly enough.

There features were all well represented in the interviews in the seventeen LEAs.

The formality of the procedures and the greater length of time taken for their accomplishment were two major factors identified as impeding efficient functioning of the procedures. The excessive length of time was attributed to three main difficulties. First was the mandatory waiting period for parental representation, although some authorities were short-cutting this process. Second was the need to take advice from all sources, which meant, in practice, inordinate delays, particularly from the medical profession. Despite the time taken for a response, the advice, when it arrived, was not always of acceptable quality, often incorporating judgemental and opinionated comment lacking in substance and couched in jargon. Third was that if the advice was to be of value it needed to be more detailed than previously, incorporating a clearer definition of needs and indications of appropriate curriculum support. However, as the Select Committee reported, and as has been indicated in earlier chapters, statements were typically thin because of resource constraints, and thus did not ensure that children's needs were met.

Such delays aggravated parental anxieties at a time when parents were already apprehensive about their role in the process. The quantity and quality of parental representations varied enormously, co-varying with the variety of practice in LEAs concerning the encouragement and assistance given to parents on their rights of representation. Too often parents were ill-informed about their rights, a problem exacerbated by the information provided by LEAs, which could be overly formal and bureaucratic, unintelligible and intimidating. The outcome was that many parents were unaware of the possibilities of provision and were not therefore in a position to make an effective judgement concerning its appropriateness. It should also be said that there appears to be, in some LEAs at least, a lack of openness with parents that is defended on the grounds of confidentiality.

Evidence from this study, and from the submissions to the Select Committee, clearly argues for a need to minimize the time between referral and placement. The suggested changes put forward by the Select Committee, some of which reflect short cuts currently in use, are for more streamlined procedures, time limits on the submission of advice, and on the whole process, and better assistance to parents to allow them to make more effective contributions, including access to a 'befriender' not employed by the local authority.

Although the Select Committee was able to state 'we are in no doubt that aspects of the present system are not working satisfactorily', the aspects it referred to were primarily administrative. It had nothing to say about the quality of integration in terms of its impact on children. HMI (1987), nevertheless, has expressed great concern: 'The quality of educational experience of those pupils with special needs, whether or not they are on statements, in ordinary schools is a particular concern.' It criticized the lack of monitoring of the effectiveness of provision for such pupils and called for evaluation as a matter of urgency. The DES (1987) has argued similarly, stating that it cannot comment on the overall effectiveness of integrated provision: some children thrive and some deteriorate; transfer to secondary schools is frequently problematic and many children have transferred from special to ordinary school at that stage.

PRACTICE

Although there are reports of successful transfer, and that 'for any degree or category of handicap we can usually find an example of education in the normal school in some part of the UK' (Booth, 1981), the most recent reviews are less than encouraging. Particularly relevant, even though it tends to relate more to North America, is that by Macmillan *et al.* (1986), who focused on mildly learning disabled children. The evidence they presented on mainstreaming indicated a social acceptance of these pupils in general but failed to provide support for the hope that mainstreaming improves their social status. Further, they found that placement in mainstream classes, without specific treatment, is likely to yield low peer acceptance for the vast majority of these children (see also Madden and Slavin, 1983). In reviewing the vast body of research in this area, they expressed concern that very little had focused on teaching, and so had failed to enlighten us much on how such children are taught or on their reactions to that teaching. They therefore agreed with Baumeister (1981), who observed that current policies on mainstreaming cannot be defended on the basis of compelling empirical evidence. The challenge, they concluded, is to study the instructional process directly. It was this challenge that we attempted to meet, in a small way, by carrying out case studies of transfer from special to ordinary schools.

The major aim of these case studies was to raise issues concerning the extent to which the children were successfully integrated, both academically and socially, not for the purpose of generalization but for the purpose of providing a clearer focus for future studies. The details of the experiences of the five children, their teachers and parents are set out in previous chapters. Table 7.1 provides a summary profile indicating the degree of success or satisfaction in relation to the major factors studied.

Table 7.1. *Profiles of pupil experiences.*

Child	Special/ ordinary school communication	Curriculum cover	Curriculum continuity	Work involvement	Appropriateness		Teacher work comments
					Language	Maths	
Jonathan	None	Very narrow	Poor	Higher in ordinary school	More difficult at ordinary	Similar	None
Timothy	None	Narrow	Poor	Higher in ordinary school	More difficult at ordinary	Similar	Of little value
Sarah	Good	Satisfactory	Adequate but little extension	Similar	Easier tasks at ordinary	Similar	Good
Peter	Good	Satisfactory	Adequate but little extension	Similar	Similar	Similar	Inadequate
Anna	Poor	Satisfactory	Poor, big overlap	Similar	Similar	Similar	Satisfactory

Psychologists, advisers and teachers all said that, if they were to cater more adequately for children with special needs, there was a need for organizational change in ordinary schools. This was also a conclusion of the Fish Report (1985), which argued strongly that the organization of secondary schools had a significant influence on the way in which special educational needs might arise. One obvious manifestation of how it arises is through the curriculum, and Hodgson (1984), among others, has found that the type of curriculum on offer is largely determined by the organizational structure of the school. This was clearly borne out in the case of the two 14-year-olds, who both experienced a very narrow curriculum. This was particularly so for Jonathan, even though the teacher had the best intentions. Attempts to adapt or scale down the ordinary school curriculum to cater for such children have frequently resulted in a narrow over-concentration on the basic skills of literacy and numeracy, which reflects the children's weaknesses, but which denies access to a wider subject cover (Hodgson, 1984). The experiences of Jonathan and Timothy certainly bear out Mortimore and Blackstone's (1982) assertion that 'there is strong evidence that disadvantaged pupils may have their choices and hence opportunities restricted' because the ordinary curriculum is unsuitable and inaccessible .

Narrow content cover was linked in Jonathan's and Timothy's cases with poor continuity of cover, an area that was barely satisfactory in the case of the other three. For the two 14-year-olds the problem was that of no overlap or clear link with their previous maths and language work, whereas with the three 11-year-olds it was more a problem of little or no development. In Anna's case there was a marked overlap. In reality, therefore, the children spent large amounts of time revising and consolidating rather than extending their knowledge and skills. No doubt part of the problem here is the lack of adequate liaison instigated by the teachers in the ordinary school, and the failure to clarify in some detail what knowledge and skills the children possessed. Ideally this information could have formed the basis of an individualized curriculum.

The work involvement of all five children was high in both types of school. However, the involvement of Jonathan and Timothy rose substantially after transfer, partly as a result of anxiety to do well, but also as a response to the didactic teaching methods usually adopted. There was little or no attempt to adapt methods to meet pupil needs more adequately, and this was reflected in teacher comments on completed work, which, with one or two notable exceptions, showed a remarkable disdain for good professional practice.

Our original fear was that the transferred children would be presented with tasks that made inappropriate intellectual demands on them. In general this fear appeared to be unjustified with those children transferring at 11, but both 14-year-olds suffered, particularly in language activities, basically because the teachers took insufficient notice of their lack of basic skills. Nevertheless, these data should be treated with caution because financial considerations limited the sample of tasks observed and their timing.

The issue of whether the children integrated successfully is a difficult one. What is apparent from this study is that it is not the child alone who determines whether or not the transfer is successful, but the interaction between the child and his or her environment. What a child has to cope with, and how he or she responds to these demands seem critical to the success of the transfer.

Socially, Jonathan, Sarah and Peter integrated very well. Only Jonathan experienced any teasing and it seemed that he was able to cope with it. For Timothy and Anna, social integration, though desired by both children, did not occur. Although the special school teacher had thought that Timothy would cope well socially in an ordinary school, he was teased and bullied and generally had a very hard time. For him this was a significant change from his classroom experience at special school where, in the opinion of his teachers, his parents and Timothy himself, he was socially accepted. In contrast, Anna's difficulties at ordinary school were simply an extension of those she had experienced in special school. Although teasing upset her, she did not let it divert her from her major goal, which seemed to be to progress academically. There was no question that she would, for example, stay away from school as a result. The difference between Anna and Timothy was one of attitude. Anna fought teasing by telling the teacher, and by arguing with those who teased her. What seemed to be a strong image of self protected her from thinking or even suspecting that her peers might be right in their treatment of her. To her the treatment was unjustified. Where she survived and Timothy fell is that he believed them to be right and Anna did not. A sweeping assessment of their integration might be that both failed. However, for Anna the fact that she had failed to integrate well socially was not a disaster, and did not seem to be proving very detrimental to her. Moreover, despite his awareness that Anna could not be said to have integrated successfully into the school, her special needs teacher felt her placement in ordinary school was an appropriate one, as did Anna's parents.

Comparing Anna and Timothy provides a good example of the 'fight or flight' syndrome. Anna fought, Timothy fled. Instead of actively dealing with the situation he simply absorbed the negative comments others made about him and withdrew from the situation. In this sense it becomes clear that the success of integration depends on how children deal with elements of the social environment they find themselves in.

The question of the success of academic integration is equally difficult. On the basis of examination results and teachers' comments, only Anna attained well compared to her peer group. Timothy and Jonathan were firmly planted at the bottom of their groups, and Sarah and Peter were near the foot of theirs. But is academic attainment the only, or indeed the best, criterion to adopt to judge academic integration? It clearly has to be taken into account, but to use it exclusively would surely be to argue that several thousand supposedly 'ordinary' children are not successfully integrated into main-stream education. The views of the children, their teachers and their parents are also salient and significant factors. Taking these into account would indicate that it was only Timothy who clearly did not integrate successfully. It is worth noting that the school to which he transferred showed the least willingness and ability to cater for individual needs. In fact it was the difference in the schools' reactions that differentiated Jonathan's experiences from those of Timothy. Although Jonathan's school could be accused of providing a restricted curriculum diet, it did create a framework within which both Jonathan and his teachers felt they could cope and build.

PARENTS

Wolfendale (1982) makes a useful distinction between treating parents as clients or as partners. In the former role they are seen as dependent on the opinions of experts, passive in the receipt of services, in need of re-education, peripheral to decision-making and in some way deficient or inadequate. In the latter role they are viewed as active participants in decision-making, as having expertise and as sharing responsibility with professionals. Regrettably, the client view is still widely held by professionals, despite increasing pressure to the contrary (Gliedman and Roth, 1981; Bookbinder, 1983).

It is clear from the parents interviewed in this study that the client view predominated. The professionals held the power to transmit information, control situations and determine outcomes, and this was bitterly resented by the parents.

Experience had taught them that to trust the wisdom and knowledge of the professional was unwise, and there was a common sense of disillusionment with the system and with the professionals who operated it. This is a sad story to relate but it should be borne in mind that the parents were, in the main, reflecting on experiences suffered several years previously. It may well be that in the intervening period some progress has been made in treating parents as partners. Let us hope so.

The parental interviews were also a rich source of information on the children's experiences after transfer, and shed light on issues and areas not illuminated by the children or their teachers. One of these issues was similar to that above, i.e. the role parents were placed in by schools. In each case parents were seen as passive receivers of information at times determined by the school. Contact was very limited, in part as a consequence of teachers' industrial action, and most contact was initiated by parents. It was quite disturbing to some parents that even when circumstances clearly demanded contact, as in Timothy's case, none was instigated.

Parents were also rightly concerned about instances of distinctly unprofessional teaching behaviour. These included: the lack of organization which allowed Timothy to spend much of his first morning at school trying to find his class base; the homework given to several of the children, which clearly and totally overestimated their capabilities; the teacher who made Timothy look a fool because he could not keep up with the pace of the lessons; the teacher who called Anna names; and the teacher who refused to justify the sex education materials being used. It would be wrong to read this as a blanket criticism of teachers. It is not, and often there were extenuating circumstances that led to the issues raised above. In Timothy's case for example, his form teacher began a long period of sick leave shortly after his arrival, and the supply teacher failed to notice Timothy's increasing absences. In addition, the parents' evening usually held was cancelled due to industrial action. Timothy's parents chose not to inform the school of his difficulties and increasingly negative attitudes, and Timothy himself chose to portray an image of 'everything is all right'. The school failed to perceive the magnitude of the situation and consequently did not take appropriate action.

It is clear from this study, and from the growing literature on parental participation, that professionals in the education service are failing to make the best use of parents' knowledge and support. Gliedman and Roth (1981) are surely correct when they argue that neither party has a monopoly on the truth, and that both must relate to each other as adults who possess complementary expertise and responsibility for the child.

Of the diverse issues that have been raised and elaborated upon in this book, the term variability best summarizes the contemporary scene. Policies relating to children with special needs vary greatly across authorities, and even within LEAs patterns of referral vary across schools. Schools within the same LEA vary markedly in provision and organization and, as the Fish Report (1985) indicated, schools have no clear view of what provision is most effective and do not receive compatible and consistent advice. Teachers within the same school also vary in the skills and motivation they bring to the teaching of children with special needs. Such skills, according to psychologists and advisers, are all too often lacking, and this leads to inappropriate curricula, diagnoses and approaches, with predictably variable results.

Most of the people interviewed and observed were performing with the best intentions within their particular constraints. But too often those intentions foundered on the rocks of implementation, with lack of resources being a strong undercurrent. However, it would be naive to think that the processes would be improved simply by throwing additional resources at them. This would not automatically inculcate more effective LEA policies, improve school organizations and teacher skills, enhance the partnership of professionals and parents or generate appropriate in-service provision. What is required is the co-ordinated effort of all professionals in the education service to achieve the common aim of providing optimal learning environments for children with special needs. We hope that this presentation of multiple perspectives on the central issues involved will, in some way, enhance the understanding necessary for that co-ordination to be effective.

Appendix

Observation Schedule

ON TASK

1. Attends to task (includes individual work, reading).
2. (a) Examines peer's work, or assists peer with work.
   (b) Peer examines target's work, or assists target.
3. (a) Initiates task talk to peer, group or class.
   (b) Attends to task talk from peer, group or class.
4. Requests help in the form of:
   (a) raising hand.
   (b) calling out.
   (c) asking for materials.
   (d) asking for instructions, demonstrations, etc.
5. Attending to teacher, in the form of:
   (a) teacher instructions, explanations or demonstrations to pupil, group or whole class.
       (b) copying from blackboard.
   6. Requesting feedback by means of:
      (a) taking work to teacher.
      (b) waiting for teacher (at desk or in queue).
   7. Organizing/fetching materials.

OFF TASK

   8. Leaves classroom.
   9. Not attending:
      (a) Passive—staring into space, wandering for no apparent reason,etc.
      (b) Aggressive—swearing, kicking, thumping, etc.
   10. (a) Initiates non-task talk to pupil, group or class.
       (b) Attends to non-task talk from pupil, group or class.
   11. Initiates non-task talk to teacher.
   12. Attends teacher non-task talk to pupil, group or class.

References

Advisory Centre for Education (ACE) (1981) *Summary of Warnock Report*. London.

Baumeister, A. A. (1981) Mental retardation policy and research: an unfulfilled promise. *American Journal of Mental Deficiency*, **85**, 449–56.

Bennett, N., Andreae, J., Hegarty, P. and Wade, B. (1980) *Open Plan Schools: Teaching, Curriculum and Design*. Windsor: NFER.

Bennett, N., Desforges, C., Cockburn, A. and Wilkinson, B. (1984) *The Quality of Pupil Learning Experiences*. London: Erlbaum Associates.

Bennett, N. and Kell, J. (1989) *A Good Start? Four Year Olds in Infant Schools*. Oxford: Basil Blackwell.

Bennett, N., Roth, E. and Dunne, R. (1987) Task processes in mixed and single aged classes. *Education 3–13*, **15**(1), 43–50.

Blankenship, C. and Lilly, M.S. (1981) *Mainstreaming Students with Learning and Behaviour Problems*. New York: Holt, Rinehart & Winston.

Bookbinder, G. (1983) Parents and professionals: what chance for a genuine partnership? Spastics Society CSIE Factsheet.

Booth, A.J. (1981) Demystifying integration. In Swann, W. (ed.), *The Practice of Special Education*. Oxford: Basil Blackwell.

Booth, A. and Potts, P. (1983) *Integrating Special Education*. Oxford: Basil Blackwell.

Cope, C. and Anderson, E. (1977) *Special Units in Ordinary Schools*. London: University of London Institute and NFER.

Cranwell, D. and Miller, A. (1987) Do parents understand professionals' terminology in statements of special educational need? *Educational Psychology in Practice*, **3**(2), 27–32.

Department of Education and Science (1981) *The School Curriculum*. Circular 6/81. London: HMSO.

Department of Education and Science (1983) *The Education (Special Education Needs) Regulations*. SI 29. London: HMSO.

Department of Education and Department of Health and Social Security (1983) *Assessments and Statements of Special Educational Needs*. Joint Circular 1/83. London: HMSO.

Dessent, T. (1987) *Making the Ordinary School Special*. Basingstoke: Falmer.

Education, Science and Arts Committee (1987) *Special Education Needs: Implementation of the Education Act 1981*. London: HMSO.

Fish Report (1985) *Educational Opportunities for All?* London: ILEA.

Galloway, D. (1985) *Schools, Pupils and Special Educational Needs*. Beckenham: Croom Helm.

Galloway, D. H. and Goodwin, C. (1979) *Educating Slow Learning and Maladjusted Children: Integration or Segregation*. Harlow: Longman.

Gliedman, J. and Roth, W. (1981) Parents and professionals. In Swann, W. (ed.), *The Practice of*

Special Education. Oxford: Basil Blackwell.

Hegarty, S., Pocklington, K. and Lucas, B. (1981) *Educating Pupils with Special Educational Needs in the Ordinary School*. Windsor: NFER-Nelson.

Her Majesty's Inspectorate (1978) *Primary Education in England*. London: HMSO.

Her Majesty's Inspectorate (1983) *9–13 Middle Schools: an Illustrative Survey*. London: HMSO.

Her Majesty's Inspectorate (1985) *Education 8–12 in Combined and Middle Schools*. London: HMSO.

Her Majesty's Inspectorate (1987) Memorandum to Education, Science and Arts Committee. London: HMSO.

Hodgson, A. (1984) Integrating physically handicapped pupils. *Special Education Forward Trends*, **11**(1), 27–9.

Kirk, S. A. and Gallagher, J. J. (1979) *Educating Exceptional Children*. Boston, MA: Houghton Mifflin.

McCall, C. (1983) *Classroom Grouping for Special Needs*. Stratford on Avon: National Council for Special Education.

Macmillan, D. L., Keogh, B. K. and Jones, R. L. (1986) Special educational research on mildly handicapped learners. In Wittrock, M. (ed.), *Handbook of Research on Teaching*. New York: Macmillan.

Madden, N. A. and Slavin, R. (1983) Mainstreaming students with mild handicaps: academic and social outcomes. *Review of Educational Research*, **53**, 519–61.

Mortimore, J. D. and Blackstone, T. (1982) *Disadvantage and Education*. London: Heinemann.

Swann, W. (ed.) (1981) *The Practice of Special Education*. Oxford: Blackwell.

Swann, W. (1985) Is the integration of children with special educational needs happening?: an analysis of recent statistics of pupils in special schools. *Oxford Review of Education*, **11**(1), 3–18.

Thomas, D. (1985) The dynamics of teacher opposition to integration. *Remedial Education*, **20**, 53–8.

Tomlinson, S. (1988) Special educational needs: the implementation of the Education Act 1981. *Journal of Education Policy*, **3**(1), 51–8.

Warnock, M. (1978) *Special Educational Needs. Report of the Committee of Enquiry into the Education of Handicapped Children and Young People*. London: HMSO.

Wedell, K., Welton, J., Evans, J. and Goacher, B. (1987) Policy and provision under the 1981 Act. *British Journal of Special Education*, **14**(2), 50–3.

Welton, J., Wedell, K. and Vorhaus, G. (1982) *The 1981 Education Act and its Implications*. Bedford Way Papers, 12. London: Institute of Education, University of London.

Wolfendale, S. (1982) Parents: clients or partners? *Journal of the Association of Educational Psychologists*, **5**, 10.

Name Index

Subject Index